GUIDE
TO THE
LEED®

GREEN ASSOCIATE
EXAM

MICHELLE COTTRELL, LEED AP

WILEY

John Wiley & Sons, Inc.

Library of Congress Cataloging-in-Publication Data:

Cottrell, Michelle.

 Guide to the LEED Green Associate (GA) Exam / Michelle Cottrell.

   p. cm. – (Wiley series in sustainable design ; 17)

 Includes index.

 ISBN 978-0-470-60829-6 (pbk.); ISBN 978-0-470-76991-1 (ebk); ISBN 978-0-470-76992-8 (ebk); ISBN 978-0-470-76993-5 (ebk)

 1. Leadership in Energy and Environmental Design Green Building Rating System–Examinations–Study guides. 2. Sustainable construction–Examinations–Study guides. 3. Sustainable buildings–Design and construction. I. Title.

 TH880.C68 2010

 720'.47076–dc22

                              2010018385

Printed in the United States of America

10 9 8 7 6 5 4 3 2 1

Contents

Acknowledgments

I WOULD FIRST LIKE TO THANK MY MOM, as I could have never completed this book without her support and for rewarding me with snacks and presents as I completed each milestone. I can never thank her enough for everything she has always done for me, for always being there for me, and being my best friend.

I would like to thank John Czarnecki, Assoc. AIA, senior editor at John Wiley & Sons, for approaching me with this opportunity and for the enormous support along the way. You have continued to have infinite faith in my abilities, for which I am extremely appreciative.

Next, I would like to thank each and every one of the image contributors, as the book would not be the same without your added visual integrity. Each of you helped to maintain my excitement about the book with your amazing images and photos.

Thank you, Zach Rose, of Green Education Services, for always being there to talk me through the organization and concepts and, most of all, for proofing the book for content. Working with you has always proven to be motivating and encouraging, as we have so much to accomplish together with GreenEDU!

I would like to thank all of my friends and colleagues for your understanding, as I "disappeared" for some months to accomplish this endeavor. Thank you to my family for granting me the time and space (especially during the holidays), allowing me to focus on this book and for even contributing some images along the way!

And, finally, Stefano Khan, how do I begin to thank you? Thank you for listening to me, making me laugh and smile, and for giving me a life outside of writing. You have continued to be an incredible support and a source of encouragement and life from the moment we met.

Introduction

Guide to the LEED® Green Associate Exam is the resource to prepare for the Leadership in Energy and Environmental Design (LEED®) Green Associate exam. This exam prep guide provides a road map to studying for the LEED Green Associate exam as administered by Green Building Certification Institute (GBCI). *Guide to the LEED Green Associate Exam* is aimed at those professionals seeking knowledge about the basic knowledge and understanding that is required in order to pass the exam and earn the LEED Green Associate accreditation.

As a means to introduce myself, I am a LEED consultant and an education provider, focused on sustainable design and building operation concepts. I have traveled the country helping many students to prepare for the LEED Green Associate and LEED Accredited Professional (AP) exams. The LEED Green Associate classes typically are one-day seminars and review all of the information as presented in this book. During these classes, I share my LEED project experiences and study tips in order to help make sense of this challenging information and present it in a logical format to help streamline the studying efforts for my students. This book breaks down the difficult information to be retained into a coherent and straightforward approach, as compared to simply repeating what would be found in the study reference material outlined by GBCI.

 Keep an eye out for these STUDY TIPS!, as they will point out the intricacies and nuances to remember.

EXAM PREP GUIDE STRUCTURE

Guide to the LEED Green Associate Exam is organized into three parts as a method to break down the information to comprehend. First, an introduction is needed to review the concepts and processes, in order to then understand the next part, the technologies and strategies to implement. Finally, the appendices include charts and diagrams summarizing the critical information, as well as other resources to narrow down the amount of information to be studied as preparation to sit for the LEED Green Associate exam. The composition of the book is as follows:

Part I: *Ramping Up is composed of the following information:*

- Chapter 1: Understanding the Credentialing Process
- Chapter 2: Introduction to the Concepts and Process of Sustainable Design
- Chapter 3: Third-Party Verification
- Chapter 4: Understanding LEED
- Chapter 5: The LEED Certification Process Summarized

 Be sure to review the eligibility requirements described in Chapter 1 to apply for the LEED Green Associate exam.

Part II: Diving In: The Strategies and Technologies of LEED details the categories that are included in the rating systems, as well as the strategies to achieve each basic concept contained within. Part II details the critical information to be retained for the exam.

In this part of the book, the following LEED categories are reviewed:

- Chapter 6: Sustainable Sites
- Chapter 7: Water Efficiency
- Chapter 8: Energy and Atmosphere
- Chapter 9: Materials and Resources
- Chapter 10: Indoor Environmental Quality
- Chapter 11: Innovation in Design and Regional Priority

Part III: Study Tips and Appendices is dedicated to summarizing the critical information, details, and concepts to retain, as well as providing an overview of the testing center environment. The appendices include additional resources to help after Part I and Part II of this book have been completed.

STUDY TIPS! are located throughout the book as tools to help stay focused on the pertinent information. They will include things to remember and point out side note type of information. Sample exam questions (in terms of format and content) are also found in the book, as well as, more basic quiz questions placed sporadically throughout.

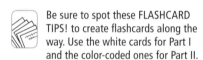

Be sure to spot these FLASHCARD TIPS! to create flashcards along the way. Use the white cards for Part I and the color-coded ones for Part II.

While reading though this book, be sure to also keep an eye out for FLASHCARD TIPS!, as they will help to depict the important aspects for the exam and act as an indicator to create critical flashcards. All of the FLASHCARD TIPS! referenced throughout the book are collected at the end, following the index, although it is suggested to make your own to enhance your studying. It is recommended to purchase plain white cards, as well as the color-coded flashcards (i.e., pink, yellow, blue, green, and purple). Use the white ones for the information to be covered in Part I and the color-coded cards for Part II of this exam prep book.

Figure I.1 Holy Wisdom Monastery project in Madison, Wisconsin, by Hoffman, LLC, reduces the amount of stormwater runoff from the site, increases the amount of open space, promotes biodiversity, reduces cooling loads, and reduces the impacts of the urban heat-island effect by implementing a vegetated roof. *Photo courtesy of Hoffman, LLC*

The FLASHCARD TIPS! suggest a starting point for flashcard creation, but feel free to make more as needed. If you decide to make your own with the help of the FLASHCARD TIPS!, be sure to refer to the flashcards at the end of the book for some additional suggestions. If you decide to use the flashcards from the end of the book you can always use markers or highlighters to color-code them if you wish.

One of the main concepts of sustainable design is the integrative fashion in which green buildings are designed and constructed. It is critical to understand how strategies and technologies have synergies and trade-offs. For example, green roofs can have an impact on a construction budget but can help save on operational energy costs, which may present a breakeven or surplus. Green roofs also have synergistic qualities, as they can help reduce the heat burden on a building, as well as help to manage stormwater. These types of concepts will be discussed in greater detail in Part II of this exam prep guide, but for now be sure to look for these BAIT TIPS! throughout Part II to help bring the concepts together.

 Be sure to look out for these Bring-All-of-It-Together Tips, which are referred to as BAIT TIPS! These tips will reinforce the important concepts and Bring All of It Together as synergies and trade-offs are pointed out for green building strategies and technologies.

STUDY SCHEDULE

Week	Chapters	Pages
1	Part I: Ramping Up (Chapters 1 through 5)	1–48
2	Part II: Sustainable Sites (Chapter 6) and Water Efficiency (Chapter 7)	49–82
3	Part II: Energy and Atmosphere (Chapter 8) and Materials and Resources (Chapter 9)	83–120
4	Part II: Indoor Environmental Quality (Chapter 10), Innovation in Design and Regional Priority (Chapter 11); Part III: Study Tips (Chapter 12)	121–150
5	Study Flashcards, rewrite your Cheat Sheet a few times, and take online Practice Exams	
6	Register and take LEED Green Associate Exam!!	

As the preceding table shows, it is recommended to read through Parts I and II of this exam prep book within four weeks. Introductory terminology from Part I should be absorbed to get on the right path to understand the more critical exam-oriented information presented in Part II. The goal is to create a complete set of flashcards during the first four weeks while reading through the material, thus allowing the following week (fifth week of studying) to focus on memorizing and studying the flashcards, followed by taking a few online practice exams which are available at GreenEDU.com.

Although the exam format and structure will be reviewed in Part III of this book, there is one component that should be revealed up front. When at the testing center and about to take the exam, there will be an opportunity to make a "cheat sheet" of sorts. Although you will not be allowed to bring any paper, books, or pencils into the exam area, you will be supplied with blank paper and a pencil (or a dry-erase board and a marker). So now that you know this opportunity is there, let's take advantage of it! Therefore, as a concept, strategy, referenced standard, or requirement is presented in this exam prep guide, make note of it on one single

 After taking some practice exams, you may want to add to your cheat sheet and/or your flashcards.

sheet of paper. At the end of Part II, this "cheat sheet" should be reviewed and then rewritten with the critical information you determine that you might forget during the exam. You are the only one who knows your weaknesses in terms of the information you need to learn—I can only make recommendations and suggestions. During Week Five, you should rewrite your cheat sheet two to three more times. The more you write and rewrite your cheat sheet, the better chance you will have for actually retaining the information. It is also advised to monitor the time it takes to generate your cheat sheet, as time will be limited on exam day.

If you maintain the recommended study schedule, four weeks from now a set of flashcards will be created and your cheat sheet started. Then you will have one week of straight studying time focused on the material in your flashcards. After studying your flashcards, it is recommended to take a few online practice exams to test your knowledge. The approach to these sample exams is described in Part III, Chapter 12, of this book, including the next steps for the cheat sheet. After a few practice exams, an assessment of your preparation should be completed to determine if you are ready for the exam. Your exam date should be scheduled at that time.

Before focusing on the exam material, be sure to read through Chapter 1 to understand the application requirements of the LEED Green Associate exam to ensure your eligibility and to understand the exam application process.

PART I

RAMPING UP

CHAPTER 1

UNDERSTANDING THE CREDENTIALING PROCESS

BEFORE DIVING INTO THE EFFORT OF STUDYING and preparing for the LEED® Green Associate exam, there are quite a few things to review to ensure your eligibility. Whenever I teach an exam prep course, this topic is not typically addressed until the end of the class, as it is easier to digest at that point; but it is important to present this information here in the first chapter, to make sure the test is applicable and appropriate for you. This chapter will provide the important concepts of the tiered credentialing system to ensure that the components, the exam application process, and the requirements for eligibility are understood.

This initial information begins with the new credentialing system for LEED accreditation, as it involves three tiers:

1. LEED Green Associate
2. LEED Accredited Professional (AP) with Specialty
3. LEED Fellow

THE TIERS OF THE CREDENTIALING PROCESS

The first step of comprehending the credentialing process begins with a brief understanding of the basics of LEED. LEED is the acronym for Leadership in Energy and Environmental Design, signifying a green building rating system designed to evaluate projects and award them certification based on their performance. The U.S. Green Building Council's (USGBC®) website indicates that LEED has become the "nationally accepted benchmark for the design, construction, and operation of high performance green buildings." USGBC created the LEED Green Building Rating System™ back in the 1990s as a tool for the public and private commercial real estate markets to help evaluate the performance of the built environment.

 Notice the LEED acronym does **not** contain an "S" at the end. Therefore, please note this first lesson: when referring to LEED, please do not say "LEEDS," as it is quite important to refer to the acronym correctly.

 Create flashcards to remember the acronyms for USGBC and LEED.

The First Tier of the Credentialing System: LEED Green Associate

The **LEED Green Associate** tier is applicable for professionals with a basic understanding of green building systems and technologies. These professionals have been tested on the key components of the LEED rating systems and the certification process. This level of credentialing is the first step to becoming a LEED Accredited Professional.

The Green Associate exam is geared toward all professionals involved in the world of sustainable design, construction, and operations, beyond just the typical architecture and engineering design professionals. Therefore, the exam is available for lawyers, accountants, contractors, owners, and developers as well. Any professional who works in the field of sustainable design and green building is eligible to sit for the exam, especially those with LEED project experience. For those who wish to sit without LEED project experience or are not employed in the field, participating in an educational course focused in sustainable design would qualify instead.

The Second Tier of the Credentialing System: LEED Accredited Professional with Specialty

The next tier, **LEED AP with Specialty**, is divided into five types (of specialties):

1. *LEED AP Building Design + Construction* (BD+C). This exam includes concepts related to new construction and major renovations, core and shell projects, and schools. This specialty will also cover retail and healthcare applications in the future.
2. *LEED AP Interior Design + Construction* (ID+C). This exam contains questions related to tenant improvement and fit-out project knowledge for commercial interior and retail professionals.
3. *LEED AP Operations + Maintenance* (O+M). This exam covers existing building project knowledge specific to operations and maintenance issues.
4. *LEED AP Homes.* This exam applies to professionals practicing in the residential market.
5. *LEED AP Neighborhood Development* (ND). This exam tests whole or partial neighborhood development project knowledge.

Because the LEED Green Associate credentialing tier is the first step to obtaining LEED AP status, the LEED AP exams are thought of in a two-part exam process beginning with the LEED Green Associate exam. You have the option to decide whether you wish to take both exams in one day or break the exam into two different testing appointments. The exams are quite challenging and mind intensive, and can be exhausting, so bear this in mind when deciding on which option to pursue.

LEED project experience is required in order to be able to sit for any of the LEED AP specialty exams. These exams cover more in-depth knowledge of each of the prerequisites and credits, the requirements to comply including documentation and calculations, and the technologies involved with the corresponding rating system. These exams are therefore applicable for those professionals working on LEED registered projects or those who worked on projects that have earned certification.

The Third Tier of the Credentialing System: LEED Fellow

Finally, the third tier of the credentialing system, **LEED Fellow**, is the highest level of credentialing, but not quite yet developed. It is meant to signify a demonstration of accomplishments, experience, and proficiency within the sustainable

TIP While there is an additional application fee to separate the LEED AP exam into two different test dates, it is still recommended to take the LEED Green Associate exam one day and take the AP specialty exam on another.

design and construction community. These individuals will have contributed to the continued development of the green building industry. The criteria for this credential are expected to be released at Greenbuild 2010, the international conference for professionals seeking more information about green building strategies.

THE APPLICATION PROCESS

Now that there is an understanding about the three tiers of the credentialing system, whom each tier is geared for, and the eligibility requirements of each exam type, it is time to review the process for applying for the exam. The first step involves visiting the Green Building Certification Institute's (GBCI's) website at www.gbci.org and downloading the *LEED Green Associate Candidate Handbook* found in the Professional Credentials section of the website.

Each of the candidate handbooks details the following information:

- Study materials—including exam format, timing, references, and sample questions
- How to apply for the exam—including the application period, eligibility requirements, and exam fees
- How to schedule your exam once your eligibility is confirmed—including confirmation, canceling, and rescheduling your test date
- A pre-exam checklist
- What to expect on the day of your exam—including name requirements, scoring, and testing center regulations
- What to do after your exam—including the Credentialing Maintenance Program (i.e., continuing education requirements) and certificates

Although the intention of this exam prep book is to consolidate all of the information needed to prepare for the LEED Green Associate exam, some of the references are updated from time to time. Therefore, this book contains similar information as found in the handbooks to add efficiency, but it is best advised to reference the latest version of the handbook appropriate to the LEED Green Associate credentialing tier for the most recent exam information.

In order to understand why a different organization (other than that of USGBC) is the resource for information for LEED professional credentials and is the destination website to apply for the exam, the role of GBCI is presented next. It is important to remember that LEED is an independent, third-party verified, voluntary rating system, and in order to be in compliance with ANSI/ISO/IEC 17024's accreditation requirements, USGBC created GBCI in order to separate the rating system development from the credentialing program. GBCI is now responsible for LEED project certification and professional credentialing, while USGBC is responsible for the development of the LEED rating systems and educating the industry for continuing efforts to help evolve the green building movement and therefore transform the market. Case in point: the USGBC website should be visited to obtain information about each rating system or to purchase reference guides, while the GBCI website should be the resource for information about taking an exam or to register a project seeking certification and learn more about the certification process.

 TIP If you are already a LEED AP, please visit www.gbci.org for more information about how the new three-tier credentialing system affects you.

 TIP GBCI updates the candidate handbooks for each of the exam types at the beginning of each month, so make sure to have the most current version.

 TIP It is not only important to refer to LEED correctly, but also to the projects and professionals involved. Remember buildings are **certified** and people are **accredited**. People will never be able to become LEED certified professionals—remember, there are LEED APs and not LEED CPs.

Additionally, LEED **certification** is meant for projects and buildings, not products. Not only will a LEED certified professional not be found, but also neither will a LEED certified chair, air-conditioning unit, appliance, paint, or glue.

It is *critical* to sign up and create the account with GBCI consistent with the account holder's name as it appears on the identification to be used to check in at the testing center. If they do not match on the day of the exam, exam fees may be lost, and the opportunity to take the exam may be forfeited. If your existing account with USGBC is not consistent with your identification, refer to the *LEED Green Associate Handbook* for instructions.

Once the handbook is downloaded and reviewed, the next step includes establishing an account with the GBCI website. If an account already exists with USGBC, the same one can be used for GBCI's website, as they are the same account. Therefore, once an account is established for GBCI, the same login information will work on USGBC's website as well. Should a new account need to be established, navigate to the "Log In to My Credentials" section of the GBCI website to create an account.

Figure 1.1 The steps to register for the LEED Green Associate exam.

APPLY!

Once an account is established with GBCI, the next step is to apply for eligibility. On the GBCI website, visit the "My Credentials" section to begin the process after logging in. Make sure the profile is correct, and select the intended credentialing path. Next, upload the documentation proving eligibility and pay the nonrefundable $50 application fee. Within seven days, you should receive an email indicating approval or not, in order to move to the next step of the exam registration process. "Five to seven percent of all applications will be audited; you will be notified immediately if you are chosen for an audit and will be notified of your eligibility within seven days."[1] Should indication be received of ineligibility, it is required to wait 90 days to apply again.

REGISTER!

The application is valid for up to one year, once approval notification is received. At this point, the next step of registering for the exam should be seen as an option within the "My Credentials" section of the website. Here, verification is required for the test to be registered for and confirmation of membership status. Remember, USGBC company members can take advantage of reduced exam fees.

SCHEDULE!

The next step is scheduling an appointment to take the exam at a Prometric testing center. As stated previously, it is advised to hold off from selecting an exam date until further along in the preparation for the exam. In the introduction of this exam prep book, a study and reading schedule is suggested. It is best recommended to start studying and determine the level of knowledge of the test content before scheduling an exam date.

When ready to schedule an exam date, please visit www.prometric.com/gbci or, if at the GBCI website, follow the links to the Prometric website to schedule a day to take the exam, from the "My Credentials" section. Remember, the eligibility code from GBCI is required to schedule an exam date. After an exam date is scheduled, a confirmation code is displayed on the screen. Keep this code! This code will be needed should the selected exam date need to be canceled, confirmed, or rescheduled with Prometric. A confirmation email will be sent from Prometric shortly after scheduling.

In addition, it is important to remember that candidates will have three allowed testing attempts per one-year application period. In the event that a retake is necessary (even though this is not the plan!), test-takers will need only to pay an additional fee for the exam and not the application fee. Refer to the *Green Associate Handbook* for more information on this rule.

> **TIP** To reschedule or cancel an exam date, please consult the *LEED Green Associate Candidate Handbook* for explicit instructions. They are quite meticulous about the procedure, so it is advised to be aware of the details to avoid risking a loss in fees paid.

WHY EARN LEED CREDENTIALS?

Just like green buildings are evaluated based on triple bottom criteria (social, economic, and environmental), deciding whether to earn LEED credentials can be approached in the same fashion, as there are individual, employer, and industry benefits to examine. From an individualistic standpoint, earning the LEED Green Associate credential will grant a professional with a differentiator to market to a potential employer or client, provide them with exposure on the GBCI website database of LEED professionals, and earn them a certificate to display and recognition as a professional on the LEED certification process. An employer would also benefit by earning the eligibility to participate on LEED projects, as more projects are requiring LEED credentials for team members; building the firm's credentials when responding to requests for proposals (RFPs) and requests for qualifications (RFQs); and having the opportunity to encourage other staff members to aim for the same credential to help the firm to evolve. Finally, the market would also benefit as more professionals earn the LEED Green Associate credential by helping the built environment to become more sustainable and the market to evolve, transform, and grow.

QUIZ TIME!

Q1.1. How many types of credentials for LEED AP with Specialty are available? (Choose one)

  A. 5

  B. 6

  C. 3

  D. 4

  E. 2

Q1.2. Is it possible to sit for the LEED Green Associate exam and the LEED AP ID+C exam in one day?

  A. Yes

  B. No

Q1.3. Is LEED project experience needed in order to sit for the LEED AP O+M exam?

A. Yes

B. No

Q1.4. Where should you go to receive the most up-to-date information on the LEED rating systems? (choose one)

A. The GBCI website

B. The ISO website

C. The USGBC website

D. The Prometric website

CHAPTER 2

INTRODUCTION TO THE CONCEPTS AND PROCESS OF SUSTAINABLE DESIGN

AS MENTIONED EARLIER, IT IS CRITICAL TO BE ON THE RIGHT PATH of understanding the basic concepts before jumping into the details of Leadership in Energy and Environmental Design (LEED®) strategies and technologies. Therefore, sustainability and green building are described and detailed as a starting point. What is *sustainability*? The Wikipedia website refers to the concept as the "the capacity to endure."[1] For the purposes of LEED, it is important to take a step further beyond sustainability and think of **sustainable design** and development. Although the definition is not universally accepted, the Brundtland Commission of the United Nations' website is cited (for the purposes of the exam and LEED) for their definition: "development that meets the needs of the present without compromising the ability of future generations to meet their own needs."[2]

Within the design industry, sustainable design and sustainable building concepts are interchangeable with the term **green building**—the next vocabulary word to become familiar with. When referring to green buildings, it is understood that the buildings are sensitive to the environment, but one might wonder how exactly? Green buildings are more efficient and use resources wisely, as they take energy, water, and materials into account (Figure 2.1). But "how do they use resources more efficiently?" one might ask. To answer this question, it is important to think of the different aspects of a building, for instance:

 Make a flashcard for the definitions of *sustainable design and development* and *green building* with your white flashcards.

- *Site selection.* Is the project a redevelopment in an urban area or does it support urban sprawl? How close is the project to public transportation to reduce the amount of cars coming and going? How will the building need to be situated in order to take advantage of the natural breezes for ventilation and daylight to reduce the need for artificial lighting within the building?

- *Design of the building systems, such as mechanical equipment, building envelope, and lighting systems.* How do they work together? Were they designed independently of each other? Is the heat emitted from the lighting fixtures accounted for? Are there gaps in the envelope that allow conditioned air to escape?

9

Figure 2.1 Reasor's Supermarket in Owassa, Oklahoma, incorporates daylighting strategies and polished concrete floors together, helping the project to earn multiple LEED credits within different categories, including Materials and Resources, Energy and Atmosphere, and Indoor Environmental Quality. *Photo courtesy of L&M Construction Chemicals, Inc.*

- *Construction processes.* Think about the people on site during construction—are they being exposed to harmful fumes and gases? Are precautions being taken to reduce the chances for mold growth or other contaminants?

- *Operations of the building.* What kind of items are purchased to support business? What about cleaning procedures?

- *Maintenance.* When was the last time equipment was tested to ensure it is performing appropriately? Are there procedures in place to monitor for leaks?

- *Waste management.* How is construction waste addressed? What about the garbage generated during operations? Is it going to the landfill? Who knows where those containers are going?!

THE BENEFITS OF GREEN BUILDINGS

> **TIP** When thinking of green buildings, it is important to think of not only how the building is designed to function and how it is constructed, but also the environmental impacts from operations and maintenance.

Hopefully, the previous questions started to generate some thoughts of what is involved with green buildings. If not, maybe evaluating the benefits of green buildings might help, beginning with a review of the traditional buildings statistics and how they impact our planet. U.S. Green Building Council (USGBC®) has compiled information from the Energy Information Administration and the U.S. Geological Survey on the impacts of buildings on our natural resources in the United States. The USGBC website reports the following statistics for *conventionally* designed and built buildings:

39 percent primary energy use

72 percent electricity consumption

38 percent carbon dioxide (CO_2) emissions

14 percent potable water consumption[3]

It is important to digest the 38 percent CO_2 emissions statistic, as this percentage puts buildings at the top of the list, followed by transportation and industry. Buildings have a bigger impact on greenhouse gas emissions—the biggest actually! These statistics have pushed the market to find better ways to design, construct, and operate buildings.

When looking at the statistics for green buildings, including LEED-certified buildings, the General Services Administration (GSA) indicates that these projects have been able to achieve the following:

26 percent energy use reduction

40 percent water use reduction

70 percent solid waste reduction

13 percent reduction in maintenance costs[4]

These percentages reflect the benefits in the economic bottom line, but these green buildings have also reduced their impact on the environment, as well as demonstrated an improved indoor environment (in terms of air quality) and contribution to the community. Indoor air quality is extremely important when analyzing the benefits of green buildings, as the Environmental Protection Agency (EPA) reports Americans "spend, on average, 90 percent or more of their time indoors."[5] Green buildings have resulted in 27 percent higher levels of satisfaction[6] and allowed students the opportunity to perform better.[7]

The Triple Bottom Line

The USGBC website summarizes the benefits of green buildings in three components: environmental, economic, and health and community benefits, as shown in Table 2.1. In the green building industry, these three concepts are defined as the *triple bottom line* (Figure 2.2). A conventional project usually assesses only the singular component of the economic prosperity for the project. However, when

Table 2.1 The Benefits of Green Buildings[8]

Environmental Benefits	Enhance and protect ecosystems and biodiversity
	Improve air and water quality
	Reduce solid waste
	Conserve natural resources
Economic Benefits	Reduce operating costs
	Enhance asset value and profits
	Improve employee productivity and satisfaction
	Optimize life-cycle economic performance
Health and Community Benefits	Improve air, thermal, and acoustic environments
	Enhance occupant comfort and health
	Minimize strain on local infrastructure
	Contribute to overall quality of life

Make a flashcard to remember the percentages of savings of green buildings.

Make flashcards to remember the triple bottom line benefits of green buildings.

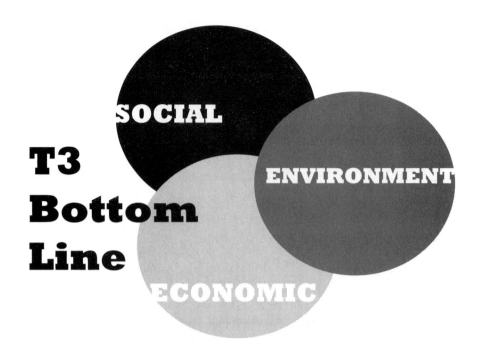

Figure 2.2 The triple bottom line.

determining the goals for a project seeking LEED certification, the process typically begins with assessing the goals in comparison to the *triple* bottom line values. For example, should a client wish to install a green roof on their building, the team would assess the financial implications as compared to the environmental impacts versus the community benefits. These types of details will be discussed later, but understanding the three types of benefits is important at this time.

QUIZ TIME!

TIP These questions are formatted just as they would be on the exam. Notice the question indicates how many answers to select. The proper number of correct answers is required on the exam, as partial credit is **not** awarded.

Q2.1. Which of the following is an environmental benefit of green building? (Choose one)

    A. Conserve natural resources

    B. Reduce solid waste

    C. Improve air and water quality

    D. Enhance and protect ecosystems and biodiversity

    E. All of the above

Q2.2. How much time, on average, do Americans spend indoors? (Choose one)

    A. 10 percent

    B. 90 percent

    C. 65 percent

    D. 35 percent

Q2.3. According to the Department of Energy's website, space heating is the largest energy use in the United States, followed by lighting. True or False?

A. True

B. False

Q2.4. Which of the following describes a high-performance green
building? (Choose one)

A. Conserves water and energy

B. Uses spaces, materials, and resources efficiently

C. Minimizes construction waste

D. Creates a healthy indoor environment

E. All of the above

THE DESIGN AND CONSTRUCTION PROCESS

The Project Team Members

Understanding the processes of design and construction, from a traditional
or conventional standpoint versus that of sustainable projects, begins with an
understanding of the players involved in the process:

Architect. Responsible for the design of green building strategies, including
overall site planning and interior spaces

MEP engineer. Responsible for the design of the energy and water systems
of a building, more specifically, the mechanical, electrical, and plumbing
components, including thermal impacts

Landscape architect. Responsible for the selection of trees and plants, the
impacts of shading, and water efficiency for irrigation; also responsible for
vegetated roof design

Civil engineer. Responsible for site design, including stormwater
management, open space requirements, and site protection

Contractor. Typically referred to as the GC, short for general contractor.
Responsible for the demolition (if required) and construction of a facility,
including site work

Facility manager. Also referred to as a building engineer. Responsible for
maintaining a building and its site during operations

Commissioning authority (CxA). Responsible for the commissioning process,
including drawing review during design and equipment installation and
performance review during construction

Owner. Defines the triple bottom line goals and selects the team members
for a project. Can be a developer and does not have to be the end user

End users/occupants. The inhabitants of a building and therefore should be
the main priority when designing for comfort and productivity

 For those not familiar with the
professionals involved, create
flashcards for each to remember
their roles and importance.

Conventional Projects versus the Integrative Design Approach

The next step to understanding the process for design and construction involves
comprehending the different types of projects, as well as the difference in the
approach of conventionally designed buildings versus the integrative approach

pursued by sustainably designed projects. Projects pursuing LEED certification are approached differently than conventional projects, as they use an integrative process that begins at the onset of the project, or as early as possible during design.

There are substantial differences between conventional and sustainably driven projects, specifically with the phases for the design and construction processes:

The Phases of the Traditional Project Delivery:

- Predesign/Programming
- Schematic Design phase
- Design Development phase
- Construction Documents phase
- Agency Permit/Bidding
- Construction
- Substantial Completion
- Final Completion
- Certificate of Occupancy

The Phases of the Integrated Project Delivery:

- Conceptualization
- Criteria Design
- Detailed Design
- Implementation Documents
- Agency Coordination/Final Buyout
- Construction
- Substantial Completion
- Final Completion
- Certificate of Occupancy

TIP Notice when all the players were introduced to the project and how they all worked in a linear and independent fashion for the traditional approach.

The key difference of the phases depends on who is involved and when, when comparing a traditionally designed and constructed building versus one that is designed with sustainable initiatives. For example, with a traditionally designed project, an owner may hire a civil or environmental team once they select a piece of property. Once the environmental reports are completed and they have an idea of how their building can fit on the site, the site plan is handed off to an architect. The architect then works with the owner to detail the program requirements (known as the **Programming** phase) and then begins to design the building (known as the **Schematic Design** phase). The architect then works with an engineering team (typically composed of mechanical, electrical, and plumbing engineers and a structural engineer, if needed, depending on the project type). These professionals typically work independently of each other to complete their tasks (known as the **Design Development** phase). Remember with a traditionally designed project, the architect has already designed the building and is now handing off the plans to the engineers to fit the building systems into the building that was designed without their input. Once the basic design elements are established, each professional works to complete a set of **construction documents** (CDs). Notice that the responsibilities are segmented just as the communication is fragmented.

What happens next with the CDs varies with different project types. Typically, these documents are first issued for permit review by the local municipality. It is quite common for most project types to send the CDs out for bid to a number of contractors about the same time as the drawings are issued for permit review (known as a Design-Bid-Build project type), while other project types have the contractor engaged as one entity with the architect from the beginning (known as a Design-Build project type).

At this point in a Design-Bid-Build project type, the contractor is given a short period of time in which to evaluate the drawings and provide the owner with a fee to provide demolition services (if required) and to construct the building, including site development work. They are given an opportunity in which they can submit questions (known as requests for information or RFIs) about the requirements or design elements during this bidding process, but then they are held to the quote they provide. Remember, the contractor was not engaged during the previous design phases, so they are not familiar with the project and have to dive in quickly, sometimes making assumptions about the construction requirements. Most of the time, projects are awarded based on the lowest bid, but think about the implications of doing so. If the lowest bidder wins the job, where are they cutting corners? Is quality being compromised? Was a critical element omitted? No one likes to lose money, as that is just bad business, but is this really the best way to select a contractor?

Once the permit is received, the contractor is selected and the construction cost is agreed upon, the phases of the design process are over and the construction process begins. Just as the design process has four phases, the construction process does as well. **Construction** commences the process, traditionally with little involvement from the design team. The next phase, **Substantial Completion**, includes the final inspection process and when the owner issues a "punch list." The owner compiles a punch list while walking the space with the contractor and notes any problems requiring the contractor's attention. **Final Completion** is next, followed by the **Certification of Occupancy**. Once the Certificate of Occupancy is received, the building is then permitted to be occupied.

When compared to the traditional project delivery method, the integrative design process for sustainable design projects involves different phases of design and construction as shown in the previous list, and remember, the main differentiator is determined by the team members, particularly how and when they are involved. For a project seeking LEED certification, the owner may engage a number of consultants early in the process to assist in selecting the property or tenant space. They may retain an architect to evaluate the site for building orientation options to capitalize on natural ventilation or daylighting opportunities. They may hire a civil engineer to research the stormwater codes and to determine access to public transportation. A LEED consultant may be engaged to assist with evaluating the triple bottom line goals particular to a project site or tenant space. Think about the benefits of bringing the landscape architect and the civil engineer on board simultaneously so they could work together to reveal the opportunities to use stormwater collection for irrigation needs. If the site were already determined, the owner would bring all of the consultants (including the general contractor) together to review the economic, social, and environmental goals collaboratively. This goal-setting meeting, or *charette,* is a key component of the first step of a sustainable project and is therefore part of the first design phase of **Programming** or **Predesign**, as the integrative process should be started as early

 TIP Besides Design-Bid-Build and Design-Build, other project delivery types are Multiprime and Construction Manager at Risk.

Make a flashcard to remember the components of an integrated project delivery (IPD).

TIP Remember, an IPD differs from a conventional project in terms of teams, process, risk, communications, agreement types, and phases.

as possible. This early start concept is graphically represented in the Macleamy Curve on page 21 of the *Integrated Project Delivery: A Guide*, as part of the recommended readings listed in the *LEED Green Associate Candidate Handbook* issued by GBCI.

Another key difference with a green building project is the use of energy modeling and Building Information Modeling (BIM). These tools allow the design team to find efficiencies and conflicts with their design intentions. They can model the proposed building systems to evaluate and predict the performance of the components specific to the elements and the project's location and site. These technologies allow the design team to specify systems and equipment sized appropriately for the specific building. Because the tools allow for the project to be evaluated from a three-dimensional perspective, design teams will also have the opportunity to find conflicts with building components and systems. The design teams can even use these tools to determine the estimated energy and water savings as compared to implementing traditional building systems. These tools are used throughout the design phases to bring more efficiency to the project for all team members.

Projects utilizing an integrative design approach bring the entire team together early in the design process, thus allowing the opportunity for everyone to work more collectively, which can actually save time and money. A project's schedule can be reduced because the project's goals are reinforced throughout every step of the process. An integrated project delivery (IPD) avoids the "value engineering" aspect that can happen on a conventionally designed project. Value engineering (VE) can take place when the bidding contractors respond with a construction cost much higher than anticipated by the owner and design professionals. In response to this high price, the design team begins to remove design elements from the original scope of work to try to get the construction cost better aligned with the project budget. IPD projects avoid this inefficiency because the contractor is evaluating the elements and drawings continuously throughout each of the design phases.

In summary, traditionally designed projects differ from IPDs in terms of teams, process, risk, communications, agreement types, and phases. Remember, conventional project teams are fragmented, whereas green building teams work more collectively. An IPD project's process is more holistically approached, while a traditional project is more linear. The risk is separated with a fragmented, traditional project as compared to an IPD. In terms of communicating ideas and concepts, traditional projects are presented in a two-dimensional format, while sustainable projects work with BIM technologies to allow the opportunity to find conflicts. Agreement types can vary, but with an IPD there is more collaboration to encourage a multilateral approach as compared to a unilateral approach of a conventional project. Finally, the phases change names from a traditional approach versus an IPD. Be sure to review Appendix H on page 163 for a comparison summary chart for traditional project delivery versus the integrative project delivery approach.

TIP Remember, with an IPD the risks may be shared across the team, but so are the rewards!

DO GREEN BUILDINGS COST MORE?

When assessing the cost of any type of project, it is important to understand the different types of costs involved. Traditionally, only two types of costs are detailed in a project's pro forma: hard costs and soft costs. Hard costs are defined as construction costs, including site work and demolition, while soft costs are related to the fees for professional services including legal and design. Soft costs also include pre- and postconstruction-related expenses, such as insurance. Green building projects take budgeting a step further by including a **life-cycle assessment** (LCA) cost. LCAs include the purchase price, installation, operation, maintenance, and replacement costs for each technology and strategy proposed to determine the appropriateness of the solution specific to the project.

TIP Chapter 9 discusses the environmental components of LCAs.

USGBC has promoted many studies, including one from Davis Langdon (as found in the primary references listed in the LEED *Green Associate Handbook*), indicating that green building does not have to cost more. This is especially true if the project starts the process early in the design phases. It is also important to bridge the gap between capital and operating budgets to understand the value of green building technologies and strategies. For example, the first or up-front cost of installing photovoltaic panels, high-efficiency mechanical systems, or an indoor water wall to improve indoor air quality may not fit in a typical budget, but if the utility cost savings were considered and evaluated, either one might make more sense. Another case in point, first costs may also be higher in a traditionally designed project because of the lack of integration. For example, a mechanical engineer may specify a larger mechanical system than what is actually needed because they may not realize that high-performance windows were specified by the architect, along with building insulation with a higher R-value. Remember, the economic bottom line is important, but a green building also evaluates the environmental and social impacts and benefits.

QUIZ TIME!

Q2.5. Risk is individually managed within an IPD. True or False?

   A. True

   B. False

Q2.6. When working on a green building project, when is the best time to incorporate an integrative design approach? (Choose one)

   A. Schematic design

   B. Construction documents

   C. Design development

   D. Beginning of construction

   E. Substantial completion

Q2.7. Life-cycle assessments (LCAs) are a beneficial tool to determine which of the following? (Choose one)

   A. Environmental benefits and potential impacts of a material, product, or technology

   B. Economics of building systems during the life of the building

   C. Environmental impacts of materials during construction

D. Social impacts of policies during a fiscal year

E. Maintenance implications, including cost, during the life of the building

Q2.8. The project team is looking to conduct a life-cycle cost analysis as a method of evaluating alternative flooring products. Which of the following should they take into consideration as inputs to that analysis? (Choose two)

A. First costs, excluding the cost of installation

B. First costs, including the cost of installation

C. Maintenance, life expectancy, and replacement cost

D. Maintenance and replacement cost, but not life expectancy

CHAPTER **3**

THIRD-PARTY VERIFICATION

WITH AN UNDERSTANDING OF THE COMPONENTS and the benefits of sustainability and green building, it is now time to take the brief information provided in Chapter 1 a bit further. In Chapter 1, Leadership in Energy and Environmental Design (LEED®) was introduced along with U.S. Green Building Council (USGBC®) and Green Building Certification Institute (GBCI). Due to the development of LEED, GBCI is able to offer third-party verification in different ways: project certification and professional credentialing. For the purposes of the Green Associate exam, it is critical to understand the following:

■ The roles, missions, and primary responsibilities of USGBC and GBCI

■ How USGBC and GBCI operate

■ The policies of USGBC and LEED

USGBC AND GBCI

Although Chapter 1 briefly introduced USGBC, it is important to remember the organization as "a 501(c)(3) nonprofit composed of leaders from every sector of the building industry working to promote buildings and communities that are environmentally responsible, profitable and healthy places to live and work," as posted on the USGBC website.[1] USGBC's mission statement is also listed on their website as "to transform the way buildings and communities are designed, built and operated, enabling an environmentally and socially responsible, healthy, and prosperous environment that improves the quality of life."[2] Remember also, USGBC created GBCI in January 2008 to "provide third-party project certification and professional credentials recognizing excellence in green building performance and practice," as indicated on the GBCI website.[3] GBCI's mission statement is stated as "to support a high level of competence in building methods for environmental efficiency through the development and administration of a formal program of certification and recertification."[4]

 Make four flashcards—two for USGBC and another two for GBCI. Two cards should include each of their mission statements and the other two cards should include each of the organizations' overviews.

Roles and Responsibilities

As indicated in Figure 3.1, USGBC is focused on developing the LEED green building rating systems, as well as providing education and research programs. In order to develop the rating systems, USGBC created a LEED Steering Committee composed of five technical advisory groups (TAGs) to help the main categories evolve. Eight regional councils are also a part of USGBC to help with the regional components of the rating systems.

 Make a flashcard to remember what a TAG is.

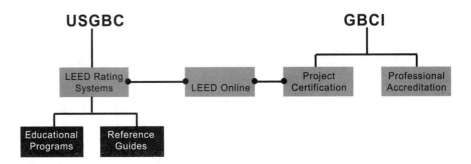

Figure 3.1 The roles of USGBC and GBCI.

Remember from Chapter 1, GBCI was created in order to separate the rating system development from the certification and credentialing process. Therefore, GBCI is responsible for administering the process for projects seeking LEED certification and for professionals seeking accreditation credentials. GBCI administers the LEED certification process for projects with the help of certification bodies. The certification bodies are responsible for managing the review process, determining a building's compliance with LEED standards, and establishing the level of certification for which they qualify. Because the certification bodies are an integral part of the certification process, they are responsible for answering and responding to **credit interpretation requests** (CIRs). For a fee, team members of registered projects seeking LEED certification can submit CIRs for clarification about a credit or prerequisite within a LEED rating system. For those in the design and construction industry, it is helpful to think of a CIR like a request for information (RFI) as described in the previous chapter. Just like a contractor may issue an RFI to the design team for clarification about a detail to be constructed, a project team can issue a CIR to their assigned certification body. For the purposes of the exam, it is important to remember that CIRs are issued specific to *one* credit or prerequisite.

Although GBCI leaves CIRs to the certification bodies to respond to and manage, they remain responsible for administering the appeals process. Team members may appeal rulings made by the certification bodies during the certification process. Ultimately, GBCI is responsible for quality assurance during the certification and credentialing process.

The Policies of USGBC and GBCI

While preparing for the exam, it is important to remember two components about USGBC, GBCI, and LEED: the proper ways to speak about each of them and the proper ways to use the many logos (also referred to as marks). There are four types of logos to be aware of: organization (USGBC, GBCI), program (LEED rating system, Greenbuild International Conference and Expo), people (accreditation earned), and project (certification level earned). For the purposes of the exam, it is crucial to remember the copyright and trademark uses for the marks, how the logos may be used, and how to properly use the terms in text. Although these guidelines are summarized here, it is advised to download the guidelines from both the USGBC and GBCI websites and review the documents.

When using any of the acronyms, it is important to define the term at the first mention. For example, in the Introduction of this guide "Leadership in Energy

TIP Be sure to check out the CIR guidelines on the GBCI website at http://www.gbci.org/Libraries/ Credential_Exam_References/ Guidelines-for-CIR-Customers.sflb.ashx

Create flashcards to remember the roles and responsibilities of USGBC and GBCI.

TIP Download the USGBC Logo Guidelines at www.usgbc.org/ ShowFile.aspx?DocumentID=3885 for more information.

Download the GBCI Logo Guidelines at www.gbci.org/Files/gbci-logo-guidelines.pdf for more information.

and Environmental Design" is mentioned for the first time and then followed by the acronym in parentheses (LEED). When using any of the logos, it is important to accompany the mark with a copyright or trademark symbol and an acknowledgment of ownership. For example, when LEED is mentioned for the first time in the introduction it is followed by a registration symbol (®). This symbol is required only at the first mention for most publications. If the LEED logo is used, it must be followed by this statement of acknowledgment of ownership by USGBC: "'LEED' and related logo is a trademark owned by the U.S. Green Building Council and is used by permission."[5] The use of any of the logos is only allowed if:

- The logo is not the largest visual component of the publication (except for chapter use).

- The logo is not used to suggest any kind of USGBC or GBCI endorsement (see copyright page of this book, for example).

- The logo is not included on any sales contracts.

- The logo is not used on any material that reflects poorly on USGBC or GBCI.

- The logo is not distorted in proportion.

- The logo is not watermarked or placed behind text.

- The logo's color is not altered (except for LEED for Homes and LEED certification logos, as detailed below).

- The logo is not accompanied by any text wrapping.

- The logo is not reduced (no smaller than 20 percent) or enlarged (no bigger than 380 percent) of its original size.

The USGBC, LEED, or GBCI logos may not be used on any product packaging, and they cannot be associated with any text indicating a claim to earn points within the LEED rating systems. The term *LEED* may be used in manufacturers' literature, as long as the material is not indicating any sort of endorsement by USGBC or GBCI. The language must indicate a holistic approach and it is not just one product that can earn points, such as:

> Products are not reviewed or certified under the LEED rating system. LEED credit requirements cover the performance of materials in aggregate, not the performance of individual products or brands. For more information on LEED, visit www.usgbc.org/leed.[6]

It is acceptable for manufacturers to use either of the following statements: "Product A contributes toward satisfying Credit X under LEED" or "Product A [complies with] X requirements of Credit X under LEED" when referring to their products.[7]

It is critical to also remember proper use of the logos and terms after a person earns professional credentials (such as LEED Green Associate) and when a project registers and earns LEED certification. After passing the exam, professionals are allowed to add "LEED Green Associate" after their name, not "LEED GA." Although a statement of ownership is required when using the legacy LEED AP mark and any of the new credentials, it is not required on business cards. In terms of projects, after registering with GBCI to indicate a project seeking LEED certification, it would be improper to indicate the level of certification when referring to the project. For example, it is unacceptable to print, "This project is LEED

Silver Registered," but it is acceptable to print, "This project is registered under the LEED Green Building Rating System." Remember also, a logo or mark does not exist for registered projects, so it is unacceptable to use one. When a project earns a level of LEED certification, team members are allowed to use the certification mark in conjunction with marketing materials for the LEED-certified project. Again, the ownership acknowledgment statement must be accompanied by the logo. Be sure to note the correct ways to refer to a certified project:

■ "LEED certification" with a lowercase "c" is used to describe the certification process.

■ "LEED certified" with a lowercase "c" is used to describe a project that has been certified.

■ "LEED Certified" with a capital "C" is used to describe a project that has been certified to the base level: Certified. When a project is certified, the correct wording is "project A is LEED Silver" or "project A is LEED certified to the Silver level" or "project A is LEED Silver certified." Due to repetition, the wording "project A is LEED Certified certified" is not recommended. "Certified" to reference both certification and level is sufficient.[8]

Finally, how the terms are used in text is another component that could be tested on the exam. As displayed throughout this book, the terms *USGBC* and *GBCI* do not include the word *the* prior to them, except if they are used as an adjective, such as "the USGBC website. ..." Be sure to note the following *unacceptable* ways to refer to USGBC:

■ U.S.G.B.C.

■ U.S. GBC

■ United States Green Building Council

■ US Green Building Council

■ GBC[9]

In any case, it is advised to receive proper permission before using any logos or statements about USGBC, GBCI, and LEED before printing or publishing any material, including websites.

QUIZ TIME!

Q3.1. Which of the following is an unacceptable way to refer to a registered project seeking LEED certification? (Choose one)

A. "Registered with the certification goal of Silver"

B. "Upon completion, this project will apply to become LEED certified"

C. "This project is registered under the LEED NC rating system"

D. "As a first step toward LEED Green Building certification, [organization name] has registered this project with the USGBC to achieve LEED certification"

E. "This project is LEED Platinum Registered"

Q3.2. Which of the following is correct? (Choose one)

    A. U.S. GBC

    B. US GBC

    C. U.S.G.B.C.

    D. U.S. Green Building Council

    E. United States Green Building Council

Q3.3. Who is responsible for the appeals process? (Choose one)

    A. GBCI

    B. USGBC

    C. Certification bodies

    D. None of the above

Q3.4. Credit interpretation requests (CIRs) provide which of the following? (Choose two)

    A. Responses to written requests for interpretation of credit requirements

    B. Determination of whether a particular strategy can be used to satisfy two different credits at once

    C. Clarification of one existing LEED credit or prerequisite

    D. Definitive assurance that a particular method or strategy permitted on a previous project will be applicable to other projects in the future

Q3.5. Which of the following statements are true in reference to certification bodies? (Choose two)

    A. Certification bodies are managed by USGBC.

    B. Certification bodies are accredited to ISO standard 17021.

    C. Certification bodies are assigned to a project once a project is registered.

    D. Certification bodies are responsible for the responding to appeals.

    E. Certification bodies help individuals prepare for their accreditation exams.

CHAPTER 4

UNDERSTANDING LEED

IN THE PREVIOUS CHAPTER, an overview of U.S. Green Building Council (USGBC®) and Green Building Certification Institute (GBCI) functions and roles was provided as a stepping-stone to understanding more about the Leadership in Energy and Environmental Design (LEED®) rating systems and the LEED certification process. In this chapter, a synopsis of the LEED rating systems will be discussed, including:

- The LEED rating systems
- The categories of LEED
- Prerequisites and credits
  - Credit weightings

Remember, the LEED rating systems were developed by USGBC as a tool to measure a building's performance. When LEED was released, there was only one generic type of rating system, where now there are quite a few to choose from for specific project types such as retail, core and shell developments, and schools. Most of the rating systems have a correlating credential under the LEED AP with specialty, as mentioned in Chapter 1. The following information is summarized in Appendix A on page 151.

THE LEED RATING SYSTEMS

LEED for New Construction and Major Renovation™ (LEED NC)

LEED for New Construction and Major Renovation (LEED NC) applies to most project types, although it was developed primarily for commercial office buildings. Other project types can include: high-rise residential buildings (4+ stories), government buildings, institutional buildings (such as libraries and churches), and hotels. This rating system can also be applied to major renovation work, including heating, ventilation, and air conditioning (HVAC) or interior rehabilitations or significant envelope modifications. With LEED NC, the owner must occupy more than 50 percent of the leasable square footage. For projects at existing facilities with a smaller scope, the LEED for Existing Buildings: Operations & Maintenance™ rating system would be more appropriate. As with any LEED rating system, it is up to the project team to determine which system is best suited to their project.

 Make a flashcard for each of the rating systems to remember what project types are best suited for each.

 TIP The majority of all LEED projects fall under the LEED NC rating system.

LEED for Schools™

The LEED for Schools rating system applies best to the design and construction of new schools, as well as existing schools undergoing major renovations. This rating system is geared toward K–12 school types and can include any project situated on the grounds of K–12 schools, such as administrative buildings, maintenance facilities, or dormitories. LEED for Schools uses the LEED for New Construction rating system as a starting point and adds classroom acoustics, master planning, mold prevention, and environmental site assessment evaluation components. For postsecondary or prekindergarten projects, the project team can determine if LEED NC or LEED for Schools is more appropriate. Existing academic buildings can look to the LEED for Existing Schools rating system.

LEED for Healthcare™

LEED for Healthcare was developed for healthcare projects including in-patient care facilities, licensed outpatient care facilities, and licensed long-term care facilities. The rating system addresses specific medical issues, such as sensitivity to chemicals and pollutants and other issues such as transportation from parking facilities and access to natural environments. Other types of medical facilities can look to this rating system, such as assisted-living facilities, medical offices, and research centers. This rating system is currently in pilot phase.

LEED Core & Shell™ (LEED CS)

 TIP The owner must occupy more than 50 percent of the leasable square footage for LEED NC projects and less than 50 percent for LEED CS projects.

LEED Core & Shell (LEED CS) was developed for the speculative development market where project teams are not responsible for all of the building's design and construction. For example, a developer may wish to build a new building but is not yet sure who will lease the interior space. Without knowing who the tenant will be, it is difficult to determine how the interior spaces will be finished and utilized. Similar to LEED NC, this rating system can be applied to commercial office buildings, medical office buildings, retail centers, warehouses, and lab facilities. The key difference between LEED NC and LEED CS relates specifically to occupancy. Remember, LEED NC requires the owner to occupy more than 50 percent of the leasable square footage, where the LEED CS rating system requires the owner to occupy less than 50 percent. Since the project team is left in the dark about the tenant(s), the rating system provides tools for guidance, such as default occupancy counts and energy modeling guidelines (specific for core and shell projects). The rating system appendix also includes tenant lease and sales agreement information specific to certification implications and LEED CS precertification guidelines.

LEED for Commercial Interiors™ (LEED CI)

The LEED for Commercial Interiors (LEED CI) rating system was developed to work hand-in-hand with LEED CS. This rating system was designed for tenants who do not occupy the entire building and therefore do not have control over the design of the building systems, including the envelope.

LEED for Retail™

LEED for Retail was developed in two different capacities depending on the type of space seeking certification: LEED for Retail: New Construction™, and LEED for Retail: Commercial Interiors™. LEED for Retail: New Construction is geared toward whole-building certification for freestanding projects, while LEED for Retail: Commercial Interiors is aimed at tenants of shopping centers and malls. Existing, freestanding retail buildings can look to the LEED for Existing Buildings: Operations & Maintenance rating system.

LEED for Existing Buildings: Operations & Maintenance™ (LEED EBOM)

The LEED for Existing Buildings: Operations & Maintenance (LEED EBOM) rating system was developed for all commercial and institutional buildings and residential buildings of four or more habitable stories. This includes offices, retail, and services establishments, libraries, schools, museums, religious facilities, and hotels. The rating system is aimed at single, whole buildings, whether multitenanted or single owner–occupied. In addition to the components of the other rating systems, LEED EBOM also encourages buildings to evaluate their exterior site maintenance programs, purchasing policies for environmentally preferred services and products, cleaning programs and policies, waste stream, and ongoing indoor environmental quality. LEED EBOM is the only certification that can expire, and therefore the only rating system that can be recertified. The program can be applicable to projects seeking certification for the first time or can apply to projects that were previously certified under another rating system, such as LEED NC, LEED for Schools, or LEED CS.

 Create a flashcard to remember the five differences of EBOM.

LEED for Homes™ and LEED for Neighborhood Development™ (LEED ND)

The next two ratings systems are structured differently than all of the other rating systems previously mentioned: LEED for Homes and LEED for Neighborhood Development (LEED ND). LEED for Homes is aimed at the residential market for dwelling units (up to three stories) with a cooking area and a bathroom. At a bigger scale, LEED ND focuses on the elements for smart growth, new urbanism principles, and sustainable building. This rating system was developed for projects including any portion of a neighborhood's design, including buildings (commercial and residential), infrastructure, street design, and open space. This rating system was created in collaboration with the Congress for New Urbanism and the Natural Resources Defense Council; therefore, projects are certified based on their ability to successfully protect and enhance the overall well-being, natural environment, and quality of life of communities and must include a residential element (new or existing).

 Remember, units with four or more habitable stories can use the LEED NC rating system, but there is also a LEED for Homes Mid-Rise rating system in pilot for buildings of four to six stories.

 LEED for Homes is the only rating system that addresses sizing a project appropriately using the Home Size Adjustment. Points are credited and deducted according to the number of bedrooms and the size of the house.

The eleven LEED rating systems are organized into five different Reference Guides for simplicity and efficiency, as opposed to individual books for each rating system. Note that some of the rating systems are still in pilot and not available to pursue for certification just yet.

THE CATEGORIES OF LEED

As mentioned earlier, LEED began as just one rating system: LEED for New Construction. As most of the other rating systems were developed, they used LEED NC as a base and therefore include the same categories. The majority of the LEED rating systems have five main categories:

- Sustainable Sites (SS)
- Water Efficiency (WE)
- Energy & Atmosphere (EA)
- Materials & Resources (MR)
- Indoor Environmental Quality (IEQ)

TIP Create a flashcard for LEED for Homes and another for LEED ND with the different categories for each.

The rating systems also include two other categories that act like bonus components: Innovation in Design (ID) (Innovation in Operations [IO] for LEED EBOM) and Regional Priority (RP). As mentioned previously, LEED for Homes and LEED ND are structured differently and therefore have different categories. LEED for Homes is also composed of two more categories in addition to the seven previously mentioned: Location & Linkages (LL) and Awareness & Education (AE). LEED ND functions differently, with only five total categories, although two should look familiar:

- Smart Location and Linkage
- Neighborhood Pattern and Design
- Green Infrastructure and Buildings
- Innovation & Design Process
- Regional Priority

QUIZ TIME!

Q4.1. A project's LEED certification can expire. True or False?

   A. True

   B. False

Q4.2. Which type of project is best suited for the LEED for Commercial Interiors rating system? (Choose one)

   A. An existing hotel renovating their HVAC system

   B. A ground-up, new construction of a school

   C. A tenant improvement project within an existing commercial building

   D. A renovation project focusing on walls, HVAC, and finishes with a 40,000-square-foot new addition

Q4.3. A developer in Phoenix is seeking LEED Gold for a new lab facility to be built in the spring. They plan on occupying 32 percent of the facility. Which rating system should they register for? (Choose one)

A. LEED for New Construction

B. LEED for Commercial Interiors

C. LEED for Existing Buildings: Operations & Maintenance

D. LEED Core & Shell

Q4.4. Which categories are specific to the LEED for Neighborhood Development rating system and not available in the other rating systems? (Choose two)

A. Sustainable Sites

B. Smart Location and Linkage

C. Innovation in Design

D. Green Infrastructure and Buildings

E. Regional Priority

Q.4.5. Which rating system addresses the appropriate sizing of a project? (Choose one)

A. LEED for Homes

B. LEED for New Construction

C. LEED for Core & Shell

D. LEED for Neighborhood Development

PREREQUISITES AND CREDITS

As shown in Figure 4.1, within each category of each of the rating systems, there are prerequisites and credits. (MPRs will be discussed in the next chapter.) It is critical to remember prerequisites are absolutely required, while credits are optional. Not all categories contain prerequisites, but all of the categories have credits. All of the prerequisites of each category, required by the majority of the rating systems, are noted in the following list. These minimum performance features will be discussed in Part II, within each chapter broken out by category. It does not matter if a project intends to pursue credits in every category—*all* prerequisites are required and are mandatory within the rating system the project is working within.

 Make a flashcard to remember the differences between credits and prerequisites. Be sure to include the following: credits are optional components that earn points, while prerequisites are mandatory, are not worth any points, and address minimum performance features.

The standard prerequisites covered in the LEED rating systems sorted by category:

Sustainable Sites
    Construction Activity Pollution Prevention

Water Efficiency
    20 Percent Water Use Reduction

Energy & Atmosphere
    Fundamental Commissioning of Building Energy Systems
    Minimum Energy Performance
    Fundamental Refrigerant Management

Materials & Resources
    Storage and Collection of Recyclables

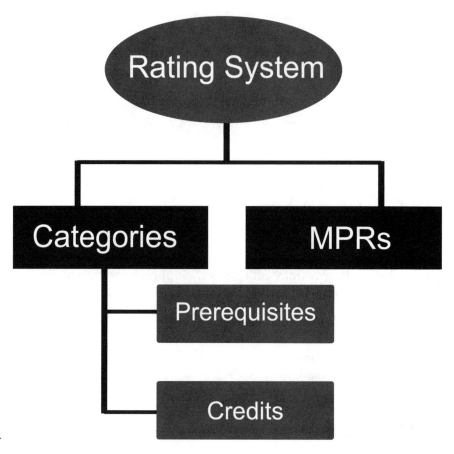

Figure 4.1 The components of a rating system.

Indoor Environmental Quality
  Minimum Indoor Air Quality Performance
  Environmental Tobacco Smoke (ETS) Control
 Each prerequisite and credit is structured the same and both include the same components.

The components of prerequisites and credits:

- Credit name and point value

- Intent—describes the main goal or benefit for each credit or prerequisite

- Requirements—details the elements to fulfill the prerequisite or credit. Some credits have a selection of options to choose from to earn point(s)

- Benefits and issues to consider—discusses the triple bottom line values to the credit or prerequisite

- Related credits—indicates the trade-offs and synergies of credits and prerequisites

- Referenced standards—lists the standard referenced for establishing the requirements of the credit or prerequisite

- Implementation—suggests strategies and technologies to comply with the requirements of the credit or prerequisite

- Timeline and team—outlines which team member is typically responsible for the credit and when the effort should be addressed

- Calculations—although most calculations are completed online, this section describes the formulas to be used specific to the credit or prerequisite

- Documentation guidelines—describes the necessary documentation requirements to be submitted electronically for certification review

- Examples—demonstrates examples to satisfy requirements

- Exemplary performance—think of these as bonus points for achieving the next incremental level of performance

- Regional variation—speaks to issues as related to project's geographic location

- Operations and maintenance considerations—describes relevance of the credit or prerequisite after building is occupied, specific to the EBOM rating system

- Resources—provides other tools or suggestions for more information on the topic

- Definitions—provides clarification for general and unique terms presented

Credit Weightings

Since prerequisites are required, they are not worth any points. All credits, however, are worth a minimum of one point. Credits are always positive whole numbers, never fractions or negative values. All credits and prerequisites are tallied on scorecards (also referred to as checklists) specific to each rating system.

 TIP Refer to the sample LEED NC scorecard in Appendix F on page 161 for a visual representation of how each category is composed of credits and prerequisites and the allocation of points.

Any project seeking certification must earn a minimum of 40 points, but this does not mean 40 credits must be awarded as well, because different credits are weighted differently and not worth only one point. To determine each credit's weight, USGBC referred to the U.S. Environmental Protection Agency's 13 Tools for the Reduction and Assessment of Chemical and Other Environmental Impacts (TRACI) categories for environmental and health concerns, including climate change, resource depletion, human health criteria, and water intake. Once the categories of impact were determined and prioritized, USGBC referred to the National Institute of Standards and Technology (NIST) for their research to determine a value for each of the credits by comparing each of the strategies to mitigate each of the impacts.

As a result of the credit weighting and carbon overlay exercise, LEED values those strategies that reduce the impacts on climate change and those with the greatest benefit for indoor environmental quality, focusing on energy efficiency and carbon dioxide (CO_2) reduction strategies. For example, transportation is a very important element within LEED, and therefore any credits associated with getting to and from the project site are weighted more. Water is an invaluable natural resource, and therefore water efficiency and consumption reduction is weighted appropriately to encourage project teams to design accordingly to use less. Providing renewable energy on a project's site will lessen the burden on fossil fuels, and therefore is also suitably weighted.

 Remember, credit weightings are based on environmental impacts and human benefits, such as energy efficiency and CO_2 reductions for cleaner air.

In summary, USGBC created a simplified, 100-base-point scale for the four different certification levels.

- Certified: 40–49 points

- Silver: 50–59 points

- Gold: 60–79 points

- Platinum: 80 and higher

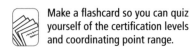

Make a flashcard so you can quiz yourself of the certification levels and coordinating point range.

The 100 base points are totaled from the five main categories: SS, WE, EA, MR, and IEQ. The last two categories make up 10 bonus points, for a total of 110 available points. LEED for Homes is structured differently, with 125 base points and 11 possible ID points.

QUIZ TIME!

Q4.6. Prerequisites are optional, depending on which categories and credits the project is pursuing. True or False?

A. True

B. False

Q4.7. A law firm occupying a 50-year-old office building is replacing the mechanical systems to improve energy performance and implementing green procurement and operations policies. Which LEED rating system best applies to this project? (Choose one)

A. LEED CI

B. LEED EBOM

C. LEED CS

D. LEED NC

E. LEED ND

Q4.8. Which of the following statements are true in regard to credit weightings? (Choose two)

A. USGBC consulted with NIST and the U.S. EPA's TRACI tool to determine the credit weightings.

B. The LEED rating systems were reorganized, and new credits were introduced to recognize what matters most, such as transportation.

C. All of the LEED rating systems are based on a 100-point scale, except for LEED for Homes.

D. All credits are worth two points within the LEED NC, but only one point within LEED CS.

Q4.9. If a university wishes to build a new administration building on their campus, they could look to LEED for New Construction or LEED for Schools rating systems and determine which one is more applicable. (Choose one)

A. True, but only if the mechanical systems are on one loop.

B. False, administration buildings cannot be certified under LEED NC.

C. True, the project team will need to determine which rating system is best suited to the project.

D. False, the university would need to look at the LEED for Universities rating system.

Q4.10. Which reference guide would you look to for information about the LEED for Schools rating system for a new, ground-up construction project you are working on? (Choose one)

    A. Reference Guide for Green Interior Design and Construction (ID+C)

    B. Reference Guide for Green Building Operations and Maintenance (GBOM)

    C. LEED for Homes Reference Guide

    D. Reference Guide for LEED Neighborhood Development

    E. Reference Guide for Green Building Design and Construction (BD+C)

Q4.11. Which of the following statements is true about credit weightings and the carbon overlay? (Choose one)

    A. Considers impact of direct energy use

    B. Considers impact of transportation

    C. Considers impact of embodied emissions of water, solid waste, and materials

    D. All of the above

Q4.12. Incorporating green building strategies, such as high-efficiency mechanical systems, on-site photovoltaic systems, and an indoor water wall to help with the indoor air quality and air conditioning, plays a role in what type of cost implications? (Choose two)

    A. Increased life-cycle costs

    B. Increased first costs

    C. Reduced construction costs

    D. Increased soft costs

    E. Reduced soft costs

Q4.13. If a project plans on earning Silver certification under the LEED for Existing Buildings: Operations & Maintenance rating system, which point range would they aim for? (Choose one)

    A. 50–59

    B. 20–30

    C. 40–49

    D. 60–69

    E. 30–39

CHAPTER **5**

THE LEED®
CERTIFICATION
PROCESS
SUMMARIZED

IN THE PREVIOUS CHAPTER, the Leadership in Energy and Environmental Design (LEED®) rating systems were introduced, including the categories, prerequisites, and credits as a starting point to understanding the process during design and construction. In this chapter, a summary of the LEED project certification process will be discussed, focusing on:

■ LEED-Online

■ Minimum program requirements

■ The certification process for projects

LEED-ONLINE

In Chapter 2, the typical project team members were defined and listed, but one component was not included: the LEED project administrator. The LEED project administrator is responsible for the coordination between all of the disciplines on the project team, by managing the documentation process once a project is registered with Green Building Certification Institute (GBCI) until certification is awarded. The LEED project administrator can be one of the team members previously mentioned in Chapter 2 and therefore would serve a dual-purpose role, or they can be an addition to the team. The administrator is typically responsible for registering a project and granting access for each of the team members to LEED-Online, the online project management system.

LEED-Online is a web-based tool used to manage a project seeking LEED certification. It is the starting point to register a project with GBCI and communicate with the certification bodies, and is used to review the documentation submitted for both prerequisites and credits during design and construction. All projects seeking certification (except LEED for Neighborhood Development™ and LEED for Homes™) are required to utilize LEED-Online to upload submittal templates and any required supporting documentation, such as drawings, contracts, and policies for review by the assigned certification body. Project teams receive reviewer feedback, can check the status of application reviews, and learn the certification level earned for their project through

 TIP To learn more about LEED-Online, be sure to check out the demo video at www.youtube.com/ watch?v=fS3yzjZxcUA.

LEED-Online. Credit interpretation requests and appeals are also processed through LEED-Online.

When a team member is invited to a project on LEED-Online, they need to login to the LEED-Online website to gain access. Once signed in, they would be greeted with the "My Projects" page to see a list of active projects they are assigned to. Once selecting one of the projects, the "Project Dashboard" page would appear. This Dashboard serves as a project's home page and gives access to:

- The project's scorecard—shows which credits the team is pursuing and their status.

- Credit interpretation rulings (CIRs).

- LEED submittal templates—think of these as the "cover pages" for each credit and prerequisite. Each of these templates summarizes how the project team has satisfied the requirements for the specific credit or prerequisite. There is a submittal template for every prerequisite and credit, which must be submitted through LEED-Online. If a calculation is needed to show compliance, the template contains a spreadsheet to complete and automatically completes the calculation after the required data is inputted, according to the requirements described in the reference guides.

- Timeline—where a project administrator would submit for certification review.

- Postcertification—to purchase plaques, certificates, and the like.

> **TIP** Remember, only invited team members can see a project's LEED-Online page, after a project is registered.

LEED for Existing Buildings

Although projects registered under the LEED for Existing Buildings: Operations & Maintenance™ (EBOM) rating system use LEED-Online just like most other LEED registered projects (except LEED for Homes and ND), there are some key differences with the process for certification. When a project is registered under the NC, CI, CS, or LEED for Schools™ rating systems, the project is certified for the design and construction of a green building. EBOM projects, however, are certified for a particular performance period. A **performance period** is a continuous period of time in which a building or facility's performance is measured. Since design-side and construction-side prerequisites and credits do not exist within the EBOM rating system, as opposed to most of the other rating systems, there is not an opportunity for design and construction reviews by the GBCI certification body. EBOM projects are submitted for certification review only after the performance period is completed.

MINIMUM PROGRAM REQUIREMENTS

> **TIP** Be sure to check out Appendix B on page 153 for an MPR summary chart.

Just as there are prerequisites that must be achieved in each rating system, there are seven minimum program requirements (MPRs) that must be met as well, in order for a project to receive certification. MPRs pertain to all the rating systems except LEED for Homes and LEED for Neighborhood Development. MPRs are critical components that are not listed on a project scorecard, but instead are confirmed when registering a project on LEED-Online. Should noncompliance with any of the seven mandated MPRs be found at any time, a project could risk losing its certification, including any fees paid for registration and certification.

The USGBC website details the seven MPRs as follows[1]:

MPR 1. Must Comply with Environmental Laws

Projects must comply with all pertinent current federal, state, and local building-related environmental laws and regulations appropriate to the particular project.

For LEED NC, LEED CS, LEED for Schools, and LEED CI Projects

This MPR must be fulfilled from the beginning of the schematic design phase until the project is awarded a certificate of occupancy.

For LEED EBOM Projects

This MPR must be fulfilled from the beginning of the performance period through the date the LEED certification expires.

MPR 2. Must Be a Complete, Permanent Building or Space

All Projects Seeking LEED Certification

All projects must be built and operated on a permanent piece of property. The project cannot be relocated at any time.

For LEED NC, LEED CS, and LEED for Schools Projects

Projects must include a new, ground-up design and construction, or major renovation, of at least one entire, all-inclusive building. Documentation may not be submitted for final review until the construction substantial completion milestone has been met.

For LEED CI Projects

The project scope must include a complete interior tenant improvement space separated from other tenant spaces within the same building by means of at least one of the following characteristics: ownership, management, lease, or party wall separation.

For LEED EBOM Projects

LEED projects must include at least one existing building, all-inclusive.

 Be sure to make flashcards to summarize and remember the seven MPRs.

MPR 3. Must Use a Reasonable Site Boundary

For LEED NC, LEED CS, LEED for Schools, and EBOM Projects

1. The LEED project boundary must include and be consistent with all of the property as part of the scope of work of the new construction or major renovation, including any land that will be disturbed for purposes during construction and operations.
2. The LEED project boundary may not include land that is owned by another party.
3. Campus projects seeking LEED certification must have project boundaries equal to 100 percent of the gross land area on the campus. If this causes a conflict with MPR 7, then MPR 7 takes precedence.

For LEED CI Projects

The LEED property boundary must include any land that will be disturbed for the LEED project.

MPR 4. Must Comply with Minimum Floor Area Requirements

For LEED NC, LEED CS, LEED for Schools, and EBOM Projects

A minimum of 1,000 square feet of gross floor area must be included in the scope of work.

For LEED CI Projects

A minimum of 250 square feet of gross floor area must be included in the scope of work.

MPR 5. Must Comply with Minimum Occupancy Rates

For LEED NC, LEED CS, LEED for Schools, LEED CI and EBOM Projects

Full-Time Equivalent Occupancy. The LEED project must be occupied by at least one full-time equivalent (FTE) occupant. If there is less than one annualized FTE, Indoor Environmental Quality (IEQ) credits will not be awarded, although compliance with IEQ prerequisites is required.

For LEED EBOM Projects

Minimum Occupancy Rate. The LEED project must be occupied and operating during the performance period, and a minimum of one year before submitting the first certification review to GBCI.

TIP Remember, all MPRs must be met in order to certify a project and to keep the certification once earned.

MPR 6. Commitment to Share Whole-Building Energy and Water Usage Data

All Projects Seeking LEED Certification

Five years of actual whole-project utility data must be shared with U.S. Green Building Council (USGBC®) and/or GBCI. For EBOM projects, this commitment begins on the day of award, and for all other rating systems, begins once the building is occupied. This data sharing must be continued even if the building or space switches ownership or lessee.

MPR 7. Must Comply with a Minimum Building Area to Site Area Ratio

All Projects Seeking LEED Certification

The project's gross floor area must be no less than 2 percent of the gross land area within the LEED project boundary.

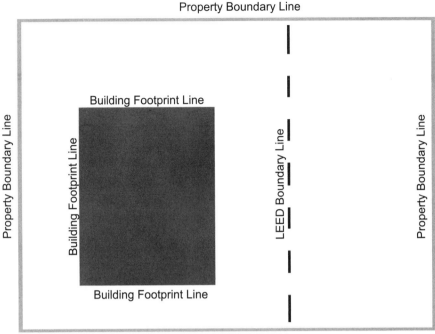

Property Boundary Line

Property Boundary Line

Building Footprint Line

Building Footprint Line

LEED Boundary Line

Property Boundary Line

Property Boundary Line

Building Footprint Line

Figure 5.1 The different types of boundaries for a LEED project.

MPR 3 refers to the LEED project boundary. There are three types of boundaries to be aware of for the purposes of LEED: property boundary line, LEED project boundary line, and the building footprint (Figure 5.1). The property boundary line refers to the land owned according to a plot plan or legal property deed. The LEED project boundary line may or may not be the same as the property boundary. For example, a university may own acres of land but may wish to develop only a portion of it for one academic building. Therefore, the LEED project boundary line sets the limits for the scope of work to be included in the documents for certification. The building footprint is the amount of land on which the building resides.

Local municipalities are responsible for establishing and determining sections of their town for different uses and therefore different zones, such as commercial, residential, and industrial zones. These sections of land are regulated based on:

■ Building type (commercial, residential, mixed-use, etc.)

■ Building height

■ Footprint, impervious vs. pervious

Project teams should be mindful of local regulations for land and the allowable uses. For the purposes of the exam, it is important to remember, although many credits may reference zoning, LEED will never override local, state, or federal requirements.

Make a flashcard to remember the three types of boundaries associated with LEED projects.

QUIZ TIME!

Q5.1. Which of the following meets the MPR regarding minimum gross floor area for the LEED for Existing Buildings: Operations & Maintenance rating system? (Choose one)

A. 250 square feet

B. 500 square feet

C. 1,000 square feet

D. 2,500 square feet

Q5.2. Which rating system has a minimum occupancy rate, in addition to the FTE occupancy, to comply with as an MPR? (Choose one)

A. LEED CI

B. LEED NC

C. LEED EBOM

D. LEED ND

Q5.3. Which of the following statements are not true in regards to MPRs? (Choose two)

A. The LEED project boundary must include all contiguous land that is associated with normal building operations for the LEED project building, including all land that was or will be disturbed for the purpose of undertaking the LEED project.

B. The owner must commit to sharing whole-building energy and water usage data for ten years.

C. LEED projects located on a campus must have project boundaries such that if all the buildings on campus become LEED certified, then 100 percent of the gross land area on the campus would be included within a LEED boundary.

D. Any given parcel of real property may only be attributed to a single LEED project building unreasonable shapes for the sole purpose of complying with prerequisites.

E. Gerrymandering of a LEED project boundary is allowed.

Q5.4. Which of the following statements are true in reference to minimum floor area requirements? (Choose two)

A. LEED NC must include a minimum of 1,000 square feet of gross floor area, while LEED CI requires a minimum of 250 square feet of gross floor area.

B. LEED NC must include a minimum of 2,000 square feet of gross floor area while LEED CI requires a minimum of 550 square feet of gross floor area.

C. LEED CS must include a minimum of 5,000 square feet of gross floor area while LEED EBOM requires a minimum of 1,000 square feet of gross floor area.

D. LEED CS must include a minimum of 1,000 square feet of gross floor area, while LEED EBOM requires a minimum of 10,000 square feet of gross floor area.

E. LEED for Schools must include a minimum of 1,000 square feet of gross floor area.

Q5.5. How many years must a project commit to sharing whole-building energy and water use? (Choose one)

A. Seven years

B. Ten years, unless the building changes ownership

C. Six months

D. One year

E. Five years

THE CERTIFICATION PROCESS FOR PROJECTS

The LEED certification process for projects begins with project registration (see Figure 5.2). To register a project, the team administrator would sign in to LEED-Online and click on the "Register New Project" tab and follow the instructions provided. The registration process begins with a review of eligibility criteria, including contact and USGBC membership verification. The next step involves selecting a rating system. LEED-Online provides assistance through a "Rating System Selector" to help the team to decipher which rating system is best suited to the specific project seeking certification. Before advancing to the "Rating System Results" step, the team administrator is prompted to confirm compliance with the seven MPRs, as described previously. After confirming MPR compliance, the applicable LEED scorecard appears. The next step of registration includes entering specific project information, including owner contact information, project address and square footage, and the anticipated construction start and end dates. All of the information is then presented on screen for review, the payment is processed, and then the registration information is confirmed. The project administrator is then awarded access to the project's LEED-Online page through their "My Projects" tab and assigned a certification body for customer service.

TIP Remember, USGBC members pay a reduced fee for project registration and certification.

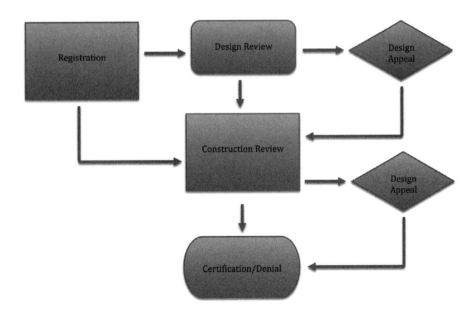

Figure 5.2 The certification review process.

TIP One team member can be assigned to more than one credit or prerequisite. Additional team members can be invited to LEED-Online and not be assigned any credit or prerequisite.

Make a flashcard to remember LPE!

TIP When a CIR is responded to by a certification body, the reply is referred to as a credit interpretation ruling.

Make a flashcard to remember the details of a CIR.

Make a flashcard to remember the three factors a project's certification fees are based on.

After a project is registered, the project administrator invites the other team members to the project's LEED-Online site and assigns each member their coordinating prerequisites and credits they will be responsible for. This means each prerequisite and credit has one responsible party assigned to it and that person will generate and upload the required documentation specific to each prerequisite and credit. When a team member is assigned a credit or prerequisite, they become the **declarant** to sign the credit submittal template. Remember, all prerequisites and credits require a submittal template, and some may require additional documentation. The additional documentation may be exempt if the design team opts to use the licensed-professional exemption (LPE) path. This optional path is determined on the submittal template.

Credit interpretation requests (CIRs, introduced in Chapter 3) can be submitted any time after a project is registered. The USGBC website contains a database of previously issued CIRs for teams to query for more information before submitting a new one, although moving forward the CIR process is changing format. For LEED 2009 projects, CIRs will become project specific and will not be posted to the database. Also, remember there is a fee associated with issuing CIRs. Note that CIR rulings are not considered final, and therefore project teams are encouraged to upload their ruling with the coordinating credit or prerequisite when submitting for a certification review with LEED-Online.

Once the design team moves through the design phase and completes the construction documents, they are allowed to submit an application for a design review, although this is optional and not required. Split reviews provide the team with a preliminary certification status to see where the project stands with point-earning potential (at least from a design prerequisite and credit standpoint). Design teams are allowed to take advantage of this split review process on all projects except for projects pursuing EBOM certification, as there is no delineation between design side or construction side prerequisites and credits within EBOM. If the team decides not to pursue this preliminary review at the end of design, they would wait to submit their documentation until after substantial completion. In summary, a project team can choose a split review for two certification reviews (one at the end of the design phase and another at the end of construction) or submit all documentation for a construction review after substantial completion.

At the time of a review submission, the LEED project administrator will need to pay a fee for certification review. This certification fee is based on the rating system the project is seeking certification with, the project's square footage, and if the project was registered under a corporate membership account with USGBC. The project administrator will be required to submit a short project narrative to provide the certification body a background of the project, the intended use of the project, the location and surrounding areas, and any other details deemed appropriate. Project photographs or renderings, elevations, floor plans, and any details should also be uploaded to LEED-Online.

The Time Frames of Certification Reviews

Table 5.1 outlines the schedule associated with the submission and review times during the LEED certification review process. Bear in mind, the time frames listed apply to both design reviews and construction reviews. Once a project team submits for either type of review, they must then wait 25 business days to

Table 5.1 Certification Review Schedule

Process	Days
Preliminary design review or construction review	25 business days
Team reply	25 business days
Final review	15 business days
Appeal (if necessary)	25 business days
Appeal review (if necessary)	25 business days
Certification awarded	

hear back from their assigned certification body. The certification body updates LEED-Online to indicate whether a credit or prerequisite is "anticipated" or "denied," or will issue clarification requests to the team specific to any credits or prerequisites in question. The team then has 25 business days to respond with more information to explain how they satisfy the requirements of the credit or prerequisite requiring clarification. At that time, the team must wait 15 business days to receive indication whether the credit or prerequisite clarified is either "anticipated" or "denied." If the team submitted for a design review, they would repeat the steps listed above at the end of substantial completion in order to submit for a construction review. It is not until this review process that the final decision to award or deny credits and prerequisites takes place.

Should the team receive a "denied" status, they can issue an appeal to GBCI for a fee within 25 business days. GBCI would then have 25 business days to review the appeal and issue a ruling to the project team. Once the appeal process ends, certification is awarded.

 Remember, GBCI is responsible for the appeals process!

LEED FOR HOMES AND LEED FOR NEIGHBORHOOD DEVELOPMENT

Just as pointed out earlier with LEED-Online and when describing the rating system categories and points, both the LEED for Homes and LEED for Neighborhood Development (LEED ND) rating systems are different from the rest. The difference this time refers to the certification process for both rating systems.

The certification process for the LEED for Homes rating system has five steps:

- Project kickoff
- Design
- Construction
- Verification
- Certification

The LEED for Homes certification process also involves different team members than previously mentioned. Besides an architect, developer, engineers, and contractor, the rating system also requires a LEED for Homes provider to help kick off the project and a green rater to perform inspections and verification during construction. The provider reviews the green rater's work and submits the documentation for review, with his or her approval. The registration and certification fees are structured differently, too, as single-family homes and multifamily housing units are priced differently.

The certification process for the LEED ND rating system is also different from the rest of the rating systems. The process involves only three steps but can take many years or even decades to complete:

■ A site plan is reviewed prior to permitting.

■ Certification is awarded based on approved plan.

■ Review is conducted after development.

PRECERTIFICATION

TIP Remember, USGBC members pay a reduced rate for registration and certification, including precertification for LEED CS projects.

Precertification is available only within the LEED for Core & Shell (LEED CS) rating system and is therefore unique. Remember, the rating system is aimed at the speculative development market, where a marketing tool is desired and beneficial. Project teams are allowed to submit, for an additional flat rate fee, for a precertification review based on declared environmental goals. Precertification is awarded based on the intentions of the project, not actual achievement of the stated goals. The review process is intended to take less than one month but can be expedited for an additional fee. Note that the precertification review fee does not include registration or regular certification review fees.

RECERTIFICATION

TIP First-time EBOM certifications are considered *initial*, and therefore projects would then need to be recertified.

Recertification is only available within the LEED for Existing Buildings: Operations & Maintenance (EBOM) rating system, and therefore is also unique. EBOM certification can be awarded to existing buildings never certified under any rating system, existing buildings previously awarded under a different rating system, or existing buildings previously awarded certification within the EBOM rating system. EBOM certifications are valid for five years, and therefore must be reapplied for and evaluated. Project teams must recertify all prerequisites but can decide to drop previously awarded credits or add new ones. Project teams also have the opportunity to decide to remain with the version of the EBOM rating system originally pursued or to opt to use a newer version of the rating system for the recertification.

QUIZ TIME!

Q5.6. Which of the following statements are true? (Choose two)

    A. Appeals are mailed to GBCI.

    B. Appeals can be submitted 25 business days after final certification review.

    C. Appeals are free.

    D. Appeals can pertain only to credits, not prerequisites or MPRs.

    E. Appeals are submitted through LEED-Online.

Q5.7. Which of the following is new to all LEED rating systems under LEED 2009? (Choose one)

A. Minimum program requirements

B. Credit interpretations requests

C. Regional Prioritization category

D. Awareness & Education category

Q5.8. Design reviews can prove to be a beneficial option for a team to pursue since the project can be awarded points before construction begins. True or False?

A. True

B. False

Q5.9. LEED project registration provides which of the following? (Choose two)

A. Three credit interpretation requests (CIRs)

B. One preapplication USGBC review of project submittals and documentation

C. One point toward LEED certification for registration prior to the development of construction documents

D. Access to online LEED credit submittal templates for the project

E. Establishment of contact with GBCI and the assigned certification body

Q5.10. An application for LEED certification must contain which of the following? (Choose two)

A. Project summary information, including project contact, project type, project cost, project size, number of occupants, estimated date of occupancy, etc.

B. A list of all members of the design and construction team, including contact information, documented green building industry experience, and indication of all LEED Accredited Professionals

C. Completed LEED credit submittal templates for all prerequisites and attempted credits, plus any documentation specifically required to support those templates

D. Detailed documentation for all credits pursued, including full-sized plans and drawings, photocopies of invoices for all purchased materials, records of tipping fees, all energy modeling inputs and assumptions, and evidence of all calculations performed in support of LEED credits

Q5.11. When should the construction credits and prerequisites be submitted for certification review? (Choose one)

A. Beginning of construction

B. One year after occupancy

    C. After substantial completion

    D. Once permit is obtained

    E. Six months after occupancy

Q5.12. Regarding the application process for LEED certification, which of the following is a correct statement? (Choose one)

    A. LEED credit submittal templates and documentation may be submitted only after occupancy.

    B. All LEED credit submittal templates and documentation must be submitted prior to construction.

    C. Prerequisites and credits marked as "Design" may be submitted and reviewed at the end of the design phase.

    D. The optional design-phase submittal allows projects to secure points for specified LEED credits, for which a preliminary certification will be awarded, if the project has earned a sufficient number of points.

Q5.13. How long does a project team have to submit an appeal after receiving certification review comments back from GBCI? (Choose one)

    A. 15 business days

    B. 25 business days

    C. 45 business days

    D. 1 week

    E. 1 month

Q5.14. Which of the following correctly characterize credit interpretation requests (CIRs)? (Choose three)

    A. Can be viewed only by the primary contact for a registered project

    B. Can be submitted any time after a project is registered

    C. Can be requested through LEED-Online

    D. Can be requested only in a written request mailed to GBCI

    E. Can address more than one credit or prerequisite

    F. Are relevant to one specific project and will not be referenced in the CIR database

Q5.15. A LEED Accredited Professional is presented with a project that was started without sustainable design or LEED certification in mind and is about to enter the construction documents phase. However, neither the owner nor any of the design team members involved thus far have significant experience with either LEED or sustainable design. Given this situation, which of the following would tend to have the most influence on the effectiveness of the sustainable design process for a project aimed at LEED certification? (Choose three)

A. Starting the sustainable design process and consideration of LEED-related goals as soon as possible

B. Extensive research, evaluation, and life-cycle assessment for intended material and technology options

C. Aggressive value engineering of individual line items to ensure that the budget is not exceeded

D. Collectively delegating responsibility for specific target LEED credits and associated strategies to appropriate team members

E. Establishing means of collaborative, interdisciplinary communication among team members as a departure from a conventionally more segmented design process

Q5.16. Which of the following rating systems do not utilize LEED-Online as means for project teams to submit documentation for certification review? (Choose two)

A. LEED NC

B. LEED ND

C. LEED for Homes

D. LEED CI

E. LEED EBOM

PART II

DIVING IN: THE STRATEGIES AND TECHNOLOGIES OF LEED

CHAPTER 6

SUSTAINABLE SITES

THIS CHAPTER BEGINS THE DETAILED STUDY OF THE STRATEGIES and technologies described within each of the Leadership in Energy and Environmental Design (LEED®) categories, starting with Sustainable Sites (SS). The main topics include the factors applicable to site selection and location, design, construction, and maintenance. As with making any other decision while working on a green building project, all components within the SS category are weighed on the triple bottom line values of environmental, economic, and community aspects.

Where a project is located and how it is developed can have multiple impacts on the ecosystem and water resources required during the life of a building. The site location can impact a building's energy performance with respect to orientation; it also could impact stormwater runoff rates or light pollution levels. How does the site fit into the existing infrastructure? Is it a contaminated site that can be remediated for redevelopment? Carbon emissions should be evaluated as well, as they could be impacted due to the transportation required to get to and from the site. Is there public transportation access available? How much parking is available for cars? Is the project site dependent on the use of cars? If so, are there incentives for carpools or vanpools? These concepts and questions should trigger some of the important factors to consider when deciding on a particular site and its true sustainable value. Once a site is selected, the project team needs to determine the most sustainable approach for development. They need to consider how much of the site will need to be developed and how much can be preserved/restored as open space. They need to work together to reduce the heat gain from the sun for the entire site, including rooftop areas. These types of site selection and site development strategies aid in the success of earning LEED certification,

 Dedicate one color flashcard for all your flashcards within the SS category. This way, anytime you see that color, you will associate that flashcard question with SS concepts and strategies.

Figure 6.1 The Los Angeles Valley College Allied Health & Sciences Center in California, by CO Architects, incorporates a stormwater retention system in the landscaping on the site and a PV system covered walkway, contributing to the achievement of earning LEED Silver certification. *Photo courtesy of Robert Canfield, CO Architects*

as proven by the project team for the Los Angeles Valley College Allied Health & Sciences Center (Figure 6.1).

To help evaluate a potential project site, the SS category within the LEED rating systems is broken down into four factors:

1. Site selection
2. Transportation
3. Site design and management
4. Stormwater management

SITE SELECTION

Determining the location of a green building project should be encouraged by previously developed locations to avoid sprawling development into the suburbs, where undeveloped (greenfield) sites would then be disturbed. The idea is to build *up* and not *out* to help increase density and reduce the negative environmental impacts of building on existing, cohesive natural habitats. Some municipalities offer an increased **floor-to-area ratio** (FAR) incentive to encourage the development of green buildings within certain communities. Zoning departments typically define building setback development lines based on the use and location of a neighborhood or town. Developers with an increased FAR allowance can build more within the setback lines and then in turn can sell more space.

From an environmental perspective, the selection of a sustainable site would avoid the destruction of wildlife habitats to help lessen the threat of the ability to survive. The goal is to preserve land and therefore preserve plant and animal species. From an economic standpoint, avoiding sprawl development helps to lessen the burden of expanding infrastructure for both utilities and transportation. The social equity of the proper site selection could include the protection of the natural environment to be enjoyed and observed by future generations for ecological and recreational purposes.

Strategies

Green buildings are encouraged to incorporate the following three strategies for proper, sustainable site selections, according to the *Green Building and LEED Core Concepts Guide*[1]:

1. *Increase density.* Maximize square footage, minimize impacts on land (Figure 6.2). Focus on **community connectivity** and **development density** concepts. **Building density** evaluates a building's total floor area as compared to the total area of the site and is measured in square feet per acre.

2. *Redevelopment.* Opt to renovate existing buildings or develop sites with access to existing infrastructure, public transportation via pedestrian access, and community services and businesses. This also includes the remediation of **brownfield** sites to improve the quality of communities and neighborhoods.

3. *Protect habitat.* Preserve wildlife and open space with minimal **site disturbance**. There is no reason to remove vegetation and trees in areas not to be developed;

Figure 6.2 Urban development in downtown Miami, Florida.

these areas should be protected and not destroyed. Also, avoid the following six types of sensitive sites:

Make a flashcard to remember the six types of sensitive sites to avoid. Make another flashcard to remember the definition of *site disturbance*: the amount of property affected by construction activity. Make two more flashcards to remember the definition for *prime farmland* and *floodplains*.

- **Prime farmland** (defined by the U.S. Department of Agriculture): Greenfield sites with soil appropriate for cultivation and agricultural growth and production.

- **Floodplains**/flood-prone areas (land less than five feet above the 100-year floodplain level as defined by the Federal Emergency Management Agency [FEMA]): Land prone to flooding as a result of a storm.

- Habitat for any endangered or critical species.

- Within 100 feet of wetlands (defined by the Code of Federal Regulations).

- Within 50 feet of a body of water (Clean Water Act).

- Public parkland.

Brownfield Sites

Make a flashcard to remember the definition of a *brownfield*: "real property, the expansion, redevelopment, or reuse of which may be complicated by the presence or potential presence of a hazardous substance, pollutant, or contaminant. Cleaning up and reinvesting in these properties protects the environment, reduces blight, and takes development pressures off green spaces and working lands."[5] Make another flashcard to remember the ASTM referenced standard for brownfield sites: E1903-97.

There are over 450,000 brownfield remediation and redevelopment opportunities in the United States available to help the reduction of sprawl developments and reuse land, thereby protecting the environment and undeveloped property.[3] These opportunities help to explain the long-term goals of the U.S. Green Building Council (USGBC®) to encourage regenerative projects. As a result of this goal, USGBC teamed with the EPA to help encourage the remediation and redevelopment of brownfield sites by rewarding more points within the LEED rating systems, therefore weighting them more than other points.[4] In order to determine if a portion of land is a brownfield site, an examination is done via the ASTM E1903-97 Phase II Environmental Site Assessment, most commonly referred to as a Phase II report. Should a site be contaminated, project teams could incorporate

Figure 6.3 Villa Montgomery Apartments, a remediation project in Redwood City, California, by Fisher-Friedman Associates, earned LEED Gold certification under the LEED NC rating system, for compliance with multiple Sustainable Sites strategies, including brownfield site selection and remediation. *Photo courtesy of Fisher-Friedman Associates*

the following common remediation strategies to clean up their project site (Figure 6.3):

- Pump-and-treat methods
- Bioreactors, land farming
- In situ (in place) remediation

QUIZ TIME!

Q6.1. What is the foundation for sustainable design for individual buildings or entire neighborhoods? (Choose one)

   A. Carbon emissions

   B. Location

   C. Water use

   D. Orientation

   E. Energy use

Q6.2. What type of assessment is used to determine brownfield sites? (Choose one)

   A. ASTM C1540 Brownfield Testing

   B. ASTM E1903-97 Phase II Environmental Site Assessment

   C. ASTM E408 Standard Test Methods for Total Emittance of Surfaces, Using Inspection Meter Techniques

   D. ASTM E789 Standard Test Methods for Evaluation for Sites

Q6.3. Which of the following types of properties is best suited for a LEED project? (Choose two)

    A. Prime farmland

    B. Floodplains

    C. Habitat for any endangered species

    D. Within 500 feet of wetlands

    E. Within 250 feet of a body of water

    F. Public parkland

TRANSPORTATION

Transportation is one of the key components addressed within the LEED rating systems, as it accounts for 32 percent of total U.S. greenhouse gas emissions in 2007, according to the U.S. Energy Information Administration.[6] As buildings traditionally have contributed to the need for transportation, green buildings have the opportunity to impact the statistics by reducing the "length and frequency of vehicle trips and encourage shifts to more sustainable modes of transportation."[7] The environmental benefits of sustainable strategies for transportation include a reduction in pollution, including vehicle emissions. Vehicle emissions have a dramatic impact on climate change, smog, and acid rain, among other air quality problems, according to Wikipedia.[8] The economic benefits include the reduction of the need to build and maintain roadways. The social component to reducing transportation impacts includes an improvement of human health, by increasing the encouragement and accessibility of walking or biking from place to place.

    The *Green Building and LEED Core Concepts Guide* indicates transportation is most impacted by four factors:

- Location—number and frequency of trips

- Vehicle technology—quantity and types of energy and support systems needed to move people and goods to and from the site

- Fuel—environmental impact of vehicle operation

- Human behavior—a daily transportation decision combining the listed impacts[9]

 TIP Vehicle technology, transportation fuels, and land use are the major contributors to transportation-contributed greenhouse gas emissions.

 TIP Land use is the ultimate contributor to the demands of transportation.

 Make a flashcard to remember the four impacts of transportation.

Strategies

Green buildings incorporate the following five strategies to help reduce transportation impacts of their sites, according to the *Green Building and LEED Core Concepts Guide*[10]:

1. *Choose a site adjacent to mass transit.* Sustainable sites provide building occupants access to public transportation (Figure 6.4).

2. *Limit parking capacity.* Sustainable buildings do not have a surplus of parking, which directly reduces impervious surfaces and encourages the use of mass transit or bicycle commuting. Reducing the amount of parking also minimizes the amount of land to be developed, therefore lowering construction costs.

Figure 6.4 Mass transit in New Jersey. *Photo courtesy of David Cardella*

Figure 6.5 Preferred parking for car/vanpool vehicles.

TIP Zero-emission vehicles (ZEVs) are standardized by California Air Resources Board (CARB).

Create a flashcard to remember the definition of an *alternative fuel vehicle*: vehicles that operate without the use of petroleum fuels, including gas-electric vehicle types. An ACEEE Green Score of at least 40 is required for compliance.

3. *Encourage carpooling.* Incentivize occupants with reserved and preferred parking spaces or a reduction in parking rates for carpools and vanpools. If more occupants participated in a ride-share program, less parking would be needed (Figure 6.5).

4. *Encourage or provide* **alternative fuel vehicles**. Building occupants should be encouraged to use low-emission vehicle types with reserved parking spaces as an incentive, or, better yet, the owners can provide hybrid or alternative fuel vehicles for occupant usage. Green buildings also have the opportunity to provide electric car recharging stations to further incentivize the use of alternative fuel vehicles.

Project teams should refer to the American Council for an Energy-Efficient Economy (ACEEE) to learn about vehicles with a minimum Green Score of 40.

5. *Alternative strategies to incentivize building users/employees.* These include reserved parking spaces or parking discounts for multioccupancy vehicles. Suppose your boss offered you cash for riding your bike to work and a place to safely store it. Would that incentivize you? What if parking rates were higher for single-occupancy vehicles—would that convince you to carpool?

Understanding these strategies when approaching a green building project allows the opportunity for project teams to evaluate the appropriateness for their specific project. But how does a team decide which strategy is appropriate and has the largest impact? Sustainable building projects utilize a variety of metrics to determine the transportation impacts associated with a specific building or a community at large. Most often, project teams use the **vehicle miles traveled** (**vmt**) metric to evaluate the demand of automobiles to commute to and from building sites. Furthermore, by the means of **transportation demand management**, project teams are able to reduce peak-period vehicle trips for their projects.

Promote Alternative Methods of Transportation

Walking helps to promote a healthier public and a more vibrant community life, and therefore is an important component addressed in the LEED rating systems.[11] The goals of sustainable buildings therefore include the promotion of commuting via bicycles or walking. Collectively, the LEED rating systems detail a credit in reference to access to transit services to relay this promotion. Within the Sustainable Sites category, points are available for projects located within a quarter-mile walk of one or more stops for two or more bus or streetcar lines or half-mile walk from rail stations, ferry terminals, or tram terminals. Projects seeking LEED certification are also awarded a point for incorporating bicycle storage (Figure 6.6) and changing rooms to help deter single-occupancy automobiles as a main source of transportation.

The most successful sustainable projects incorporate a multitude of strategies to lessen the burden of commuting to and from building sites. Green buildings promote walking and provide bicycle storage to reduce the use of automobiles.

Make a flashcard to remember the five strategies to reduce the transportation impacts associated with buildings.

If more people carpooled, walked, or biked to work or school, there would be less pollution.

TIP Remember, vehicle miles traveled is the metric with the *best* indicator of transportation impacts associated with the construction of a new building or neighborhood.

TIP Remember quarter-mile bus or half-mile rail.

TIP Co-commuting reduces the total vehicle miles traveled.

Figure 6.6 Bike racks at the Animal Care and Protective Services Facility in Jacksonville, Florida. *Photo courtesy of Auld & White Constructors, LLC*

TIP Single-passenger vehicles are more energy intensive than mass transportation.

They reduce the amount of parking and provide incentives for occupants who decide to forgo the single-occupancy vehicle commute. Selecting a project site in an urban area with a higher density is typically serviced by existing mass transit, therefore reducing the need for commuting via car. Continuously choosing urban infill sites and avoiding sprawl is expected to result in a larger reduction in greenhouse gas emissions, as opposed to technological and alternative fuel advancements for vehicles. For LEED ND projects, the project teams design communities to reduce the number and length of trips required by automobiles.

LEED for Neighborhood Development

Create a flashcard to remember the definition of *street grid density:* the number of centerline miles (length of a road down the center) per square mile.

Of the various LEED rating systems, LEED for Neighborhood Development™ has the largest ability to impact the mind-set of commuting and the behavior of travel and, therefore, the largest impact to reduce the transportation impacts associated with buildings (Figure 6.7). LEED ND project teams are encouraged to expand the three strategies of site selection as discussed earlier, to the scale of a neighborhood and not just one building's site. Since the rating system promotes pedestrian access and walking as a primary means of transportation, LEED ND project teams should evaluate a neighborhood's **street grid density** to determine a neighborhood's

Figure 6.7 Baldwin Park in Orlando, Florida, incorporates multiple bike paths throughout the community to encourage the use of bicycles as a method of transportation in lieu of automobiles. *Photo courtesy of Baldwin Park Development Company*

density and therefore, how pedestrian friendly it is. The rating system further encourages this strategy by encouraging the **diversity of use and housing types** to promote walking and for the residents to become less dependent on cars. A diversity of businesses and community services allows an integration of uses to minimize the length of travel. A diversity of housing types supports a variety of household types, ages, sizes, and income levels to cohabitate in the same neighborhood.

 Create another flashcard to remember the definition of *diversity of use and housing types:* the variety of building uses and housing types per acre.

QUIZ TIME!

Q6.4. Which of the following street grid density descriptions promotes a more pedestrian friendly community? (Choose one)

   A. A higher street grid density with narrow streets interconnecting

   B. A higher street grid density with wide streets interconnecting

   C. A lower street grid density with wide streets interconnecting

   D. A lower street grid density with narrow streets interconnecting

Q6.5. Which of the following represent the major factors that impact transportation effects on the environment? (Choose three)

   A. Vehicle technology

   B. Fuel

   C. Human behavior

   D. Quality of roads

   E. Suburban development

Q6.6. Which of the following are sustainable strategies that should be implemented on an auto-dependent green building? (Choose four)

   A. Provide priority parking for carpools/vanpools.

   B. Provide a mass transit discount program to employees.

   C. Supply alternative fuel vehicles and accessibility to recharging stations.

   D. Offer discounted parking rates for multioccupant vehicles.

   E. Incorporate basic services (such as a bank, gym, cleaners, or pharmacy) for occupant usage in the new building.

Q6.7. Which of the following are effective and sustainable strategies to address transportation for a LEED project? (Choose three)

   A. Choose a site near a bus stop.

   B. Limit parking.

   C. Encourage carpooling.

   D. Provide SUVs for all employees.

   E. Choose a greenfield site.

SITE DESIGN AND MANAGEMENT

 Create two flashcards to remember each of the definitions for *native and adaptive plantings* and *potable water*.

 TIP **Xeriscaping** can also be used as a sustainable landscaping strategy, as it uses drought-adaptable and minimal-water plant types along with soil covers, such as composts and mulches, to reduce evaporation.

 Create a flashcard to remember the definitions of *imperviousness*: surfaces that do not allow water to pass through them; and *perviousness*: surfaces that allow water to percolate or penetrate through them.

 Create another flashcard to remember the definition of *stormwater runoff*: rainwater that leaves a project site flowing along parking lots and roadways, traveling to sewer systems and water bodies.

Once a building's site is selected, site design and management become the next components to address when working on a green building project. Project teams are encouraged to utilize the concepts of sustainable landscaping techniques, including **native and/or adaptive plantings** and water-efficient irrigation systems. Native plantings refer to native vegetation that occurs naturally, while adaptive plantings are not natural but can adapt to their new surroundings; both can survive with little to no human interaction or resources. They should select plants that will not only require less water and maintenance, but also improve the nutrients in the soil and deter pests at the same time. Implementing these measures reduces the amount of chemicals in the water infrastructure, and therefore improves the quality of surface water and saves building owners from purchasing fertilizers and pesticides. Avoiding or reducing the amount of **potable water** (drinking water supplied by municipalities or wells) used for irrigation, decreases the quantity of water required for building sites and therefore reduces maintenance costs as well.

Sustainable sites should also address two other components: minimizing **impervious**, or hardscape, surfaces such as parking lots and paved walkways, and utilizing optimized exterior lighting schemes within their site designs. Impervious surfaces ultimately contribute to **stormwater runoff** and therefore decrease the quality of surface water and reduce groundwater recharge (Figure 6.8). In terms of site lighting, traditionally there has been little attention paid to the quality of the night sky and the effects on wildlife, or to the wasteful

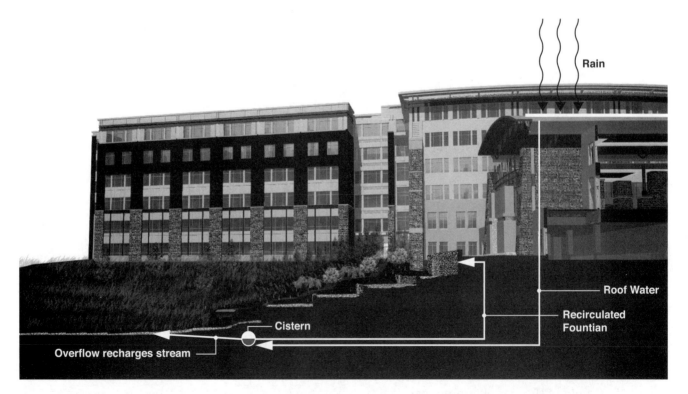

Figure 6.8 Dick's Sporting Goods Corporate Headquarters in Pittsburgh, Pennsylvania, designed by Strada Architecture, LLC, incorporates roof water capture to reduce the stormwater runoff and reduce the need for potable water for irrigation. *Photo courtesy of Strada Architecture LLC*

energy use approach for exterior lighting. It is inefficient to illuminate areas not used at night, light areas beyond a property's boundary, or overcompensate light levels, or **footcandle** levels. If footcandle levels are minimized, light pollution is reduced, dark night skies are preserved, and nocturnal animal habitats remain unaffected.

Although energy use will be discussed in more detail in Chapter 8, materials used for site design and rooftops can efficiently impact the use of energy for two reasons. Think of summertime at the grocery store parking lot and how you can see heat emitting from the black asphalt surface. The sun is attracted to darker surfaces, where heat is then retained. Multiply this effect in a downtown, urban area to understand the true impacts of urban **heat island effect**. By specifying and implementing materials with a high **solar reflectance index (SRI)**, green building projects can reduce the heat island effect and the overall temperature of an area. A material's SRI value is based on the material's ability to reflect or reject solar heat gain measured on a scale from 0 (dark, most absorptive) to 100 (light, most reflective). Building materials are also evaluated based on their ability to reflect sunlight based on visible, infrared, and ultraviolet wavelengths on a scale from 0 to 1. This solar reflectance is referred to as albedo; therefore, the terms *SRI* and *albedo* should be thought of synonymously.

If a lighter roofing material is used, the mechanical systems do not have to compensate for the heat gain to cool a building, therefore reducing the use of energy (Figure 6.9). If high-SRI materials are used for surface paving, walkways, and rooftops, light can be distributed more efficiently at night to reduce the number of light fixtures required, which saves money during construction and, later, during operations (Figure 6.10).

Project teams are encouraged to create natural, sustainable exterior environments that can be sustainably maintained to add to the economic, environmental, and social equity of their green building projects.

 Create another flashcard to remember the definition of a *footcandle*: a measurement of light measured in lumens per square foot.

 Create another flashcard to remember the definition of *heat island effect*: heat absorption by low-SRI, hardscape materials that contribute to an overall increase in temperature by radiating heat.

 Create a flashcard to remember the definition of **emissivity** as described in the EBOM rating system: "the ratio of the radiation emitted by a surface to the radiation emitted by a black body at the same temperature."[12]

 Create two more flashcards to remember the definition of solar reflectance index (SRI) and albedo. Remember the difference scales for each.

 Besides low-albedo, nonreflective surface materials, car exhaust, air conditioners, and street equipment contribute to the heat island effect, while narrow streets and tall buildings can serve to further exacerbate the problem.

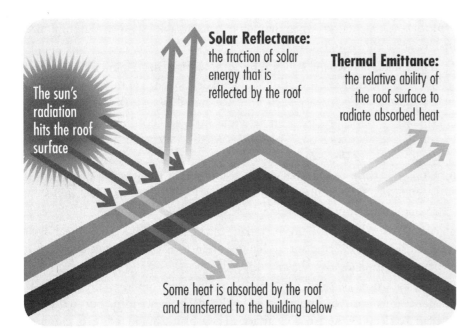

Figure 6.9 Diagram illustrating solar reflectance and thermal emittance. *Image courtesy of Cool Roof Rating Council*

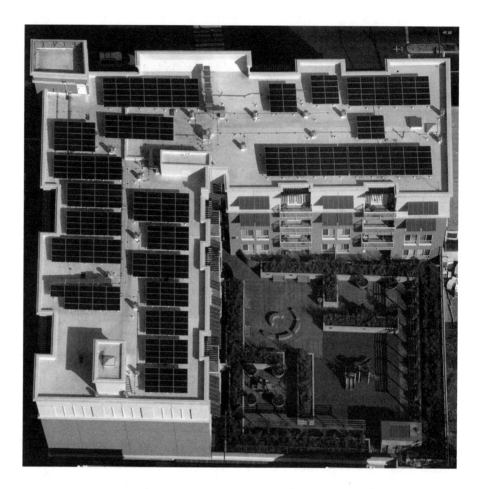

Figure 6.10 The roof at Villa Montgomery Apartments in Redwood City, California, reduces the urban heat island effect by the installation of a combination of a high solar reflectance index (SRI) roof material with photovoltaic systems (generating a portion of the electricity needed for operations), along with a green roof, including a playground that offers residents the opportunity to enjoy the outdoor environment. *Photo courtesy of Fisher-Friedman Associates*

Create another flashcard to remember the definition of *building footprint*: the amount of land the building structure occupies not including landscape and hardscape surfaces such as parking lots, driveways, and walkways.

Tuck-under parking helps to reduce impervious surfaces, reduces the impacts of the urban heat island effect, reduces runoff, and helps to preserve open space for parking and nonparking uses.

Strategies

There are six core strategies that address these site design concepts to be considered for implementation when designing a sustainable site that also minimizes maintenance efforts and costs[13]:

1. *Build small.* Reduce the size of a **building's footprint** (Figure 6.11), increase the FAR, and decrease the amount of land developed, and therefore maximize the amount of open space. If parking is required, use a tuck-under approach.

2. *Minimize hardscape.* These impervious surfaces contribute to stormwater runoff and therefore carry pollutants to the water stream, decreasing the quality of water (Figure 6.12).

3. *Minimize water usage.* In terms of site design, using native and adaptive vegetation and/or utilizing a high-efficient irrigation system reduces the amount of water needed.

4. *Use reflective materials.* Using materials with high SRI can reduce the heat island effect (Figure 6.13) and spread light at night for a cost-effective approach to exterior lighting.

5. *Develop a sustainable management plan.* Not only should an integrated pest management plan be implemented by the maintenance team, but so should a plan for cleaning the exterior surfaces. These plans should reduce or eliminate

Figure 6.11 The high-efficiency Duke Law Star Commons project in Durham, North Carolina, by Shepley Bulfinch, obtained its LEED Certification by providing access to public transportation and reducing site disturbance and the heat island effect. *Photo courtesy of Kat Nania, Shepley Bulfinch*

Figure 6.12 Turfstone™ Open-Grid Pavers allow stormwater to pass through, in order to recharge groundwater and reduce runoff. *Photo courtesy of Ideal*

Figure 6.13 The Yale Arts Complex project in New Haven, Connecticut, designed by Gwathmey Siegel & Associates Architects, reduces the urban heat island effect by incorporating roof materials with high SRI. *Photo courtesy of Gwathmey Siegel & Associates Architects*

 TIP Light trespass is the unwanted light shining on another's property.

 Create a flashcard to remember the six strategies to address for site design and management.

 It is the collective strategies that have the biggest reduction of building-associated environmental impacts, such as tuck-under parking with reserved spaces for low-emitting fuel types and carpools/vanpools. Remember the synergies of green building strategies.

chemicals and waste that could flow into the water stream and therefore decrease the water quality. The plan should also address energy and water usage to avoid waste, as well as other pollution reduction methods.

6. *Reduce light pollution.* Exterior light fixtures should project light down, not up toward the night sky (Figure 6.14). Minimal light levels should be maintained at night for safety for parking lots and walkways, but what about areas not occupied at night?

Figure 6.14 The Utah Botanical Center's Wetland Discovery Point building at Utah State University in Kaysville was mindful of the nocturnal environment in which the center resides by providing very minimal exterior lighting and shielding any fixtures that would pollute the night sky. *Photo courtesy of Gary Neuenswander, Utah Agricultural Experiment Station*

QUIZ TIME!

Q6.8. Which of the following is the best landscape design strategy to implement to reduce heat island effects? (Choose one)

A. Absorption

B. Xeriscaping

C. Increased albedo

D. Deciduous trees

E. Increased imperviousness

Q6.9. The owner of a two-story office project has suggested that he is interested in the installation of a vegetated roof system and would like the design team to evaluate it as an option. Which set of team members best represents all of those who might offer meaningful input to this evaluation? (Choose one)

A. Architect, landscape architect, and civil engineer

B. Architect, contractor, and structural engineer

C. Landscape architect, contractor, civil engineer, and structural engineer

D. Architect, structural engineer, landscape architect, and civil engineer

E. Architect, structural engineer, landscape architect, civil engineer, and mechanical engineer

F. Architect, structural engineer, landscape architect, civil engineer, mechanical engineer, and contractor

Q6.10. Emissivity is an indication of which of the following material properties? (Choose one)

A. Ability to reflect light from light sources

B. Ability of a transparent or translucent material to admit solar gain

C. Ability of a material to absorb heat across the entire solar spectrum, including all nonvisible wavelengths

D. Ability of a material to give up heat in the form of long-wave radiation

Q6.11. The design team has attempted to address 50 percent of the hardscape surfaces on the project's site to meet the requirements to reduce the heat island effect for LEED compliance. Which of the following strategies should the LEED Accredited Professional discuss with the design team? (Choose three)

A. Effective tree-shaded area of hardscape features

B. Solar reflectance index for all nonstandard paving materials proposed

C. Percentage of perviousness for proposed open-grid paving materials

D. Emissivity of all low-albedo hardscape features in the design

E. Runoff coefficients for impervious paving materials selected

STORMWATER MANAGEMENT

In the previous section, strategies were presented to address while designing a sustainable site, including the importance to reduce the amount of impervious surfaces. One benefit of minimizing impervious surfaces is the reduction of stormwater runoff, which causes degradation of the quality of surface water and reduces groundwater recharge to the local aquifer. The reduction in surface-water quality is caused by both a filtration decrease and the increase of hardscape areas containing contaminants. The increase of impervious surfaces and stormwater runoff has put water quality, aquatic life, and recreational areas at risk.

Nonpoint source pollutants, such as oil leaked from cars or fertilizers from plantings, are one of the biggest risks to the quality of surface-water and aquatic life. These pollutants typically contaminate rainwater flowing along impervious surfaces on the journey to sewer systems or water bodies, especially after a heavy rainfall. Once this rainwater is in the sewer system, it then contaminates the rest of the water and takes a toll on the process to purify it or it contaminates the body of water into which it is dumped. These bodies of water also then suffer from soil erosion and sedimentation, deteriorating aquatic life and recreational opportunities. Therefore, allowing rainwater to percolate and penetrate through **pervious** surfaces, such as pervious concrete, porous pavement, or open-grid pavers, reduces the pollution of surface water and is less of a burden on our eco-system. For projects located in urban areas where space is limited, oil separators can be utilized to remove oil, sediment, and floatables. Within an oil separator, heavier solid materials settle to the bottom while floatable oil and grease rise to the top.

Project sites could also include other strategies to reduce runoff including **wet** or **dry ponds**. Both of these approaches utilize excavated areas used to detain rainwater from leaving the site and therefore slow runoff. Two other options include on-site filtration methods. **Bioswales,** or engineered basins with vegetation, can be utilized to increase groundwater recharge and reduce peak storm-water runoff (Figure 6.15). The other option, **rain gardens**, functions to collect and filter runoff while reducing peak discharge rates. Rooftops also contribute to the pollution of surface water, so implementing a green, or vegetated, roof would also reduce stormwater runoff. The best environmental strategies include treating all surface water before allowing it to leave the site. For example, the Rivers Casino project team designed the site so that all surface water flows through a series of catchment areas that promote plant growth as a means to filter the water before it enters the riverbank (Figure 6.16).

The triple bottom line benefits of managing stormwater include preserving the natural ecological systems, such as wetlands that promote **biodiversity** and help manage stormwater (see Figure 6.17). If the natural environment is already

TIP Nonpoint source pollutants are one of the biggest risks to the quality of surface water and aquatic life.

 Reducing the amount of impervious surfaces, and increasing pervious surfaces, helps to reduce stormwater runoff and therefore also helps to save the quality of water.

Figure 6.15 Bioswales, an on-site filtration strategy, can help to recharge the groundwater and reduce stormwater runoff. *Photo courtesy of Thomas M. Robinson, EDR*

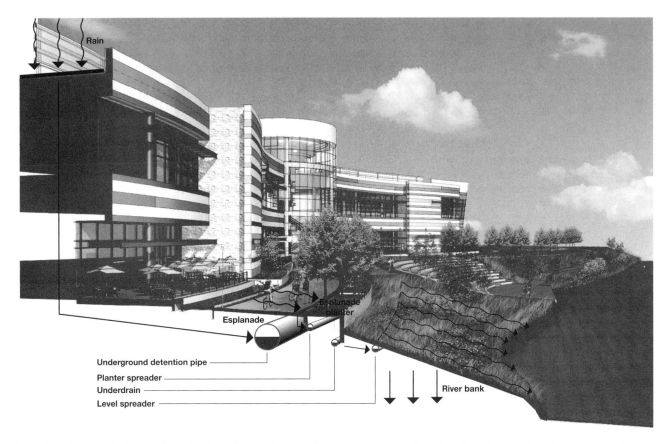

Figure 6.16 Rivers Casino Riverfront Park in Pittsburgh, Pennsylvania, addresses stormwater quantity and quality by incorporating filtration measures to capture and clean rainwater. *Photo courtesy of Strada Architecture, LLC*

Figure 6.17 The Utah Botanical Center's Wetland Discovery Point project, at Utah State University in Kaysville, earned LEED Platinum certification for its efforts to create biodiversity. *Photo courtesy of Gary Neuenswander, Utah Agricultural Experiment Station*

able to manage stormwater, we could take advantage of the economic savings of not creating manmade structures to do it for us, as well as the costs to maintain the structures. There is also social equity in managing runoff and maintaining clean surface water: the preservation of aquatic life and the ability to enjoy recreational activities.

Strategies

For the purposes of the LEED Green Associate exam, it is important to remember three strategies in particular for managing stormwater[14]:

1. *Minimize impervious areas.* Remember open-grid pavers, porous paving, pervious concrete, and green roofs to increase pervious surfaces (Figure 6.18).
2. *Control stormwater.* Remember rain gardens, dry ponds, and bioswales slow down runoff while allowing the natural environment to infiltrate and clean the water of pollutants.
3. *Harvest rainwater.* Collect it and use it later for nonpotable uses, such as irrigation, custodial uses, and flushing toilets and urinals, but be mindful of local rules and regulations (see Figure 6.19).

 Green roofs have many synergies, including maximizing open space, creating a habitat for wildlife, and reducing stormwater runoff and the heat island effect, but they also help to insulate a building and therefore reduce energy use. The trade-offs with green roofs include installation cost and maintenance.

 Create a flashcard to remember the three strategies to address stormwater management.

QUIZ TIME!

Q6.12. Which of the following are strategies to reduce stormwater runoff? (Choose three)

A. Green roofs

B. Impervious asphalt

C. Pervious pavers

D. Bioswales

Figure 6.18 This green roof at the Allegany County Human Resources Development Commission's community center in Cumberland, Maryland, minimizes impervious areas to reduce stormwater runoff. *Photo courtesy of Moshier Studio*

Figure 6.19 Stormwater is collected on-site and stored in cisterns at the Utah Botanical Center's Wetland Discovery Point building and used to flush toilets, as well as irrigate the site, therefore reducing the need for potable water. *Photo courtesy of Gary Neuenswander, Utah Agricultural Experiment Station*

Q6.13. A vegetated roof system using native and adapted plant species has the opportunity to contribute to earning which three credits? (Choose three)

A. Rapidly Renewable Materials

B. Stormwater Design: Quantity Control

C. Heat Island Effect

D. Low-Emitting Materials: Composite Wood & Agrifiber Products

E. Optimize Energy Performance

Q6.14. Which of the following are LEED concepts that are *most* significantly influenced by site selection prior to design of the project? (Choose two)

   A. Heat Island Effect

   B. Alternative Transportation: Low-Emitting and Fuel-Efficient Vehicles

   C. Alternative Transportation: Public Transportation Access

   D. Minimize Water Usage

   E. Brownfield Redevelopment

Q6.15. How many basic services are required to comply with the LEED rating systems?

   A. 5

   B. 4

   C. 12

   D. 10

   E. 6

Q6.16. What is the minimum required American Council for an Energy-Efficient Economy (ACEEE) score for low-emitting and fuel-efficient vehicles by the LEED rating systems?

   A. 100

   B. 40

   C. 10

   D. 5

   E. 20

Q6.17. What material options would be best to comply with the LEED rating systems for roofing materials? (Choose two)

   A. Gray asphalt with an SRI of 22

   B. Aluminum coating with an SRI of 50

   C. Red clay tile with an SRI of 36

   D. White ethylene propylene diene monomer (EPDM) with an SRI of 84

   E. White cement tile with an SRI of 90

   F. Light gravel on built-up roof with an SRI of 37

CHAPTER 7

WATER EFFICIENCY

THIS CHAPTER FOCUSES ON THE STRATEGIES and technologies described within the Water Efficiency (WE) category of the Leadership in Energy and Environmental Design (LEED®) rating systems, including methods to reduce the consumption of water, our most precious resource that is often taken for granted. As the demand for water continues to increase and supplies are decreasing, it is challenging for municipalities to keep up. The U.S. Geological Survey estimates that buildings account for 12 percent of total water use in the United States. Potable water that is delivered to buildings and homes is first pulled from local bodies of water, treated, and then delivered. This water is typically used for toilets, urinals, sinks, showers, drinking, irrigation, and for equipment uses, such as mechanical systems, dishwashing, and washing machines. Once the wastewater leaves the building or home, it is treated and then delivered back to the body of water. When the influx supersedes the capacity of the wastewater treatment facilities, overflow will result. This overflow can pollute and contaminate nearby water bodies, the sources of potable water, therefore causing the need for more treatment facilities to be built. Therefore, it is critical to understand how to reduce the amount of water we consume, to reduce the burden on the entire cycle, especially as we are threatened with shortages in the near future.

Green building design teams have the opportunity to specify efficient fixtures, equipment, and appliances that require less water. They also have the ability to implement rainwater-harvesting technologies to capture nonpotable water to use for multiple applications inside and out. In order to capture stormwater, runoff is collected from a roof and stored in a cistern on site (Figure 7.1). Each of the three uses of water detailed in this chapter include strategies for nonpotable water uses to reduce consumption.

Not only is it important to reduce the amount of potable water that is required from the utility companies, but green buildings also have the opportunity to reduce the amount of wastewater that leaves a project site. Implementing biological wastewater treatment technologies can be cost prohibitive, so teams are encouraged to assess the return on investment (ROI) through the means of triple bottom line evaluation.

Building and site designs can help to reduce the amount of water that is required for operations and the amount of wastewater that leaves a site. Water efficiency for green buildings is addressed in three components:

1. Indoor water use
2. Outdoor water use (for irrigation)
3. Process water

Once these efficiency strategies are implemented to reduce the amount of water required, it is also important to monitor consumption and note any inefficient occurrences, such as leaks.

Remember to pick a new color for flashcards created for the Water Efficiency category topics.

Create a flashcard to remember the three types of water uses described in the Water Efficiency category. Remember, Appendix D summarizes all of the strategies of each category to remember for the exam.

Water efficiency helps to reduce energy and therefore costs by reducing the amount of water that must be treated, heated, cooled, and distributed.

Figure 7.1 Capturing and storing rainwater to use for irrigation reduces the need for potable water. *Photo courtesy of Rainwater HOG, LLC*

Similar to the strategies discussed within the Sustainable Sites category, there are triple bottom line values to water-efficient strategies. From an environmental standpoint, the more we build with impervious surfaces, the harder it is for the groundwater to recharge naturally. From an economic viewpoint, the more we contribute to sprawl, the more we increase the demand for more facilities and additional distribution systems to be built at a cost to the public. In addition, the energy required to heat water is in direct comparison to the amount of water used; use less hot water, use less energy, save money. Although the social equity of water is drastically understated, as its economic value does not reflect its importance, maintaining clean sources of water is imperative to future generations. The Utah Botanical Center's Wetland Discovery Point project earned Platinum level certification for addressing each of the triple bottom line components for the project (Figure 7.2).

When approaching the strategies to reduce water for a project seeking LEED certification, it is necessary for the project teams to calculate a **baseline** for water

Figure 7.2 The Utah Botanical Center's Wetland Discovery Point project is located within a natural habitat requiring the team to address environmental impacts as a result of the new construction, such as water quality. In order to earn its Platinum certification the team utilized a trombe wall as a thermal mass to capture the heat from the sun during the day and release it at night for heating. *Photo courtesy of Gary Neuenswander, Utah Agricultural Experiment Station*

usage versus what the project is intended to require. The WE prerequisite and each of the credits utilizes the Energy Policy Act of 1992 (EPAct 1992) for flow and flush rates associated with conventional and efficient fixtures (see Table 7.1). Project teams should also reference the Energy Policy Act (EPAct) of 2005, as it became U.S. law in August 2005.

Create a flashcard to remember the Energy Policy Act of 1992 (EPAct 1992) as the standard for all WE prerequisites and credits.

Once the fixture water consumption is determined, project teams need to account for the occupant usage to calculate how much water is required for the building. The full-time equivalent (FTE) occupancy is an estimation of actual building occupancy in terms of hours occupied per day and is used to determine the number of occupants for the building that will use the fixtures. FTE is calculated by dividing the total number of occupant hours spent in the building (each full-time employee is assumed to be in the building for eight hours) divided by eight. Therefore, full-time employees have a value of one. Part-time employees must also be considered in the calculations, if they work four hours a day, they have a value of 0.5. If a building has 100 occupants, 50 of whom work full time and 50 of whom work part time, the FTE for the project is 75. It is also important to remember to include transient occupants in occupancy calculations. For example, if a project team were designing a library, they would need to account for the visitors to the library, as well as the staff and employees. These visitors are thought of as transient occupants for the purposes of LEED.

TIP Notice that FTE is the acronym for *full-time* equivalent and not *full-time employee*. Make sure you account for part-time and transient occupants as well!

Create a flashcard to remember baseline versus design: the amount of water a conventional project would use as compared to the design case.

Table 7.1 Water Consumption Assumptions According to EPAct 1992

Fixture Type	Gallons per Flush (gpf)
Conventional water closet (for baseline calculations)	1.6
Low-flow water closet	1.1
Ultra-low-flow water closet	0.8
Composting toilet	0.0
Conventional urinal (for baseline calculations)	1.0
Waterless urinal	0.0

A low-flow water closet uses 30 percent less water than a conventional water closet.

INDOOR WATER USE

Indoor water use typically includes the water used for water closets, urinals, lavatories, and showers. Break room or kitchen sinks are also included in the calculations for indoor water use. For the purposes of the exam, it is important to understand and remember the differences between a flush fixture and a flow fixture and how their consumption is measured. Flush fixtures, such as toilets and urinals, are measured in **gallons per flush** (gpf). Flow fixtures, such as sink faucets, showerheads, and aerators, are measured in **gallons per minute** (gpm).

The LEED rating systems define potable water use as an important component that green buildings should address and therefore require a reduction in consumption as a minimal performance feature. This importance is characterized by the means of a prerequisite within the WE category. Therefore, LEED-certified projects must demand at least 20 percent or less indoor water as compared to conventionally designed buildings.

Strategies

Keeping within the lines of the basic concept to use less water, efficient indoor water strategies help to change the typically traditional, wasteful behavior of occupants. Project teams should conduct life-cycle cost assessments for determining the best solution for their projects. For example, waterless urinals might cost less to install,

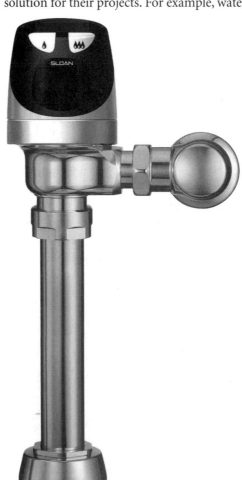

as they do not require water, but their maintenance costs might be higher than a conventional fixture. Overall, most of these strategies will not be noticeable, but will substantially reduce water consumption:

1. *Use efficient plumbing fixtures* such as low-flow toilets, showerheads, and faucets (Figure 7.3). Some teams go a step further and install waterless fixtures, such as toilets and urinals (Figure 7.4). Automatic faucet sensors and metering controls should also be considered. When existing fixtures cannot be replaced, buildings should employ flow restrictors and sensors on flow fixtures.

2. *Use nonpotable water* for flush functions for toilets and urinals, including captured rainwater (Figure 7.5), **graywater**, and municipal reclaimed water.

3. *Install submeters* to track consumption and monitor for leakage.[1]

 Create flashcards to remember flow and flush fixture types and how they are measured.

 Water efficiency strategies incorporated into site design, such as collecting rainwater on-site, can help to reduce the demand for indoor water for flush fixtures.

 Create a flashcard to remember the definition of graywater: wastewater from showers, bathtubs, lavatories, and washing machines. This water has not come into contact with toilet waste according to the International Plumbing Code (IPC).

TIP Wastewater from toilets and urinals is considered **blackwater**. Kitchen sink, shower, and bathtub wastewater is also considered sources of blackwater. Remember, it's not the source that matters, but what could be in it! For example, washing machine wastewater could be considered blackwater, as it is used to wash cloth diapers.

 Create a flashcard to remember the three strategies for indoor water use.

Figure 7.3 Using high-efficiency faucets and high-efficiency toilet (HET) fixtures and Flushometers, which use 1.28 gpf or less, helps to achieve the water reduction prerequisite of 20 percent. *Photo courtesy of Sloan Valve Company*

Figure 7.4 Waterless urinals help to reduce the indoor water consumption. *Photo courtesy of SmithGroup, Inc.*

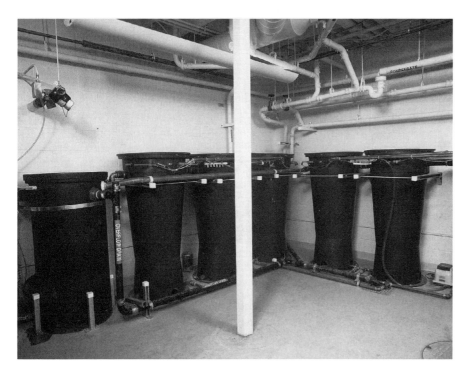

Figure 7.5 Stormwater is collected for reuse to reduce the need for potable water at the Natural Resources Defense Council's Robert Redford Building in Santa Monica, California. *Photo courtesy of Grey Crawford*

QUIZ TIME!

Q7.1. If an existing building seeks water efficiency strategies but has a limited budget, installing which of the following would be economically viable options? (Choose two)

    A. Aerators

    B. Low-flow toilets

    C. Waterless urinals

    D. Capturing rainwater for irrigation

    E. Flush valves

Q7.2. Which of the following products are not examples of a flow fixture? (Choose two)

    A. Lavatory faucets

    B. Toilets

    C. Sprinkler heads

    D. Aerators

    E. Showerheads

    F. Urinals

OUTDOOR WATER USE FOR IRRIGATION

Water used for irrigating landscaping accounts for the primary use of outdoor water usage, and is therefore a component to be addressed and reduced in green buildings. Remembering the concepts discussed in the previous chapter, site design including native and adaptive plants can drastically reduce the amount of water required for irrigation, if not eliminate the need for irrigation all together (Figure 7.6). If irrigation is required, implementing a high-efficiency system can also substantially reduce the amount of water required over conventional designs. Green building projects might also implement other sustainable options, including capturing rainwater to use for irrigation and indoor water flush functions.

Remember, both composting and mulching optimize soil conditions to add to the efficiencies of native and adaptive plantings and high-efficiency irrigation systems.

Chapter 6 introduced the heat island effect and how it is responsible for an overall temperature increase of an area. Combining the impacts of greenhouse gas emissions, the heat island effect, and increased impervious surfaces from sprawling developments, water is thus evaporating at quicker rates and not getting delivered to plants and vegetation. Project teams need to be aware of these conditions and plan accordingly, efficiently, and sustainably. To calculate the amount of water actually delivered to vegetation by the proposed irrigation system and not blown away or evaporated, a project team determines the **irrigation efficiency** of the proposed system. For the purposes of the exam, it is important to remember what the team members need to consider as part of the calculations, not necessarily how they calculate factors, such as irrigation efficiency.

The amount of water delivered by sprinkler heads is measured in gallons per minute (gpm).

Figure 7.6 Native and noninvasive plantings do not require irrigation or fertilizers.

Strategies

Pulling together the concepts and strategies from the Sustainable Sites (SS) category, such as native planting and xeriscaping, and repeating a couple from indoor water use, the outdoor water use strategies include[2]:

1. *Implement native and adapted plants*—requires little to no maintenance. Drought-resistant plants are the *best* environmental option!

2. *Use xeriscaping,* combining native planting with soil improvements and efficient irrigation systems (Figure 7.7).

3. *Specify high-efficiency irrigation systems*—moisture sensors included! Types include surface drip, underground, and bubbler systems.

4. *Use nonpotable water,* specifically for irrigation. Includes captured rainwater, graywater, and municipal reclaimed water (Figure 7.8).

5. *Install submeters* to track consumption and monitor for leakage.

 Remember the strategies discussed in the previous chapter. Proper site design will help to reduce water consumption for landscaping needs. Reducing water demands affects both the SS and WE categories.

 Create a flashcard to remember the five strategies for outdoor water use.

Figure 7.7 Xeriscaping helps to reduce the need for potable water for irrigation.

QUIZ TIME!

Q7.3. Which of the following strategies might contribute to water-efficient landscaping? (Choose three)

A. Planting of hardwood trees to provide shade

B. Planting native or adapted plant species

C. Installing turf grass

D. Reducing amount of pervious surface area

E. Combining vegetated swales and cisterns to capture rainwater

Figure 7.8 Collecting and storing stormwater for reuse helps to reduce the burden on the local municipality. *Photo courtesy of Rainwater HOG, LLC*

Q7.4. A previously developed site is undergoing a major renovation. The plans include avoiding undeveloped areas and planting more than half of the site area with native and adapted vegetation. Retention ponds and bioswales will also be implemented with native vegetation. Which of the following LEED concepts might these design strategies contribute? (Choose four)

A. Heat island effect

B. Stormwater runoff reduction

C. Site disturbance

D. Water-efficient landscaping

E. Increase density

Q7.5. The major renovation of a four-story, 40,000-square-foot building in Florida includes repaving existing parking areas along the entire length of the south and west facades of the building. The building and parking areas compose the entire site to its boundaries, not leaving any green space. The common afternoon rain showers have led the design team to select open-grid paving with vegetated cells equivalent to 50 percent of its surface in lieu of a lower-first-cost solution, such as black asphalt. Based on the information provided, which of the following benefits and LEED strategies might the open-grid paving strategy contribute? (Choose three)

A. Reduced site disturbance
B. Water-efficient landscaping
C. Heat island effect
D. Stormwater management
E. Optimize energy performance
F. Water use reduction

PROCESS WATER

Create a flashcard to remember the uses for process water.

TIP A cooling tower "uses water to absorb heat from air-conditioning systems and regulate air temperature in a facility."[3]

The types of water use reduction intentions previously described may be more obvious strategies for green buildings as opposed to the third type: process water. Water used for building systems, such as heat and cooling air, is considered process water. Process water is used for industrial purposes, such as chillers, cooling towers, and boilers, and also includes water used for business operations, such as washing machines, ice machines, and dishwashers.

Building managers and owners should be aware where water is required and how much is consumed at those specific locations. Green building design teams know efficient building systems require less water. Taking advantage of closed-loop systems allows buildings to extend the use of water in a contaminant-free environment. Installing meters to understand the demands of water for building systems and how much is consumed could help economically, specifically in terms of cooling tower makeup water. This water is evaporated during the operation of a cooling tower and, if metered, could be an opportunity for credit from the utility company, as it does not enter the sewer system, which would then need to be treated.

TIP ENERGY STAR–certified appliances, such as washing machines and dishwashers, are energy efficient and require less process water.

Create a flashcard to remember the three strategies to address process water use.

Remember the sources of nonpotable water, including capturing rainwater, to reduce the demands for the many outdoor, indoor, and process water uses. See the end of the book for flashcard examples.

Strategies

Building managers can reduce the amount of water required for building system and operation needs by incorporating the following strategies[4]:

1. *Use efficient equipment and appliances* such as boilers, chillers, and cooling towers.

2. *Use nonpotable water* for building systems. Remember, this includes captured rainwater, graywater, and municipal reclaimed water.

3. *Install submeters* to track consumption and monitor for leakage.

QUIZ TIME!

Q7.6. Which of the following are types of process water uses?
(Choose three)

   A. Cooling towers

   B. Boilers

   C. Washing machines

   D. Cisterns

   E. Toilets

Q7.7. Which of the following are potential sources of nonpotable
water? (Choose three)

   A. Blackwater

   B. Municipally supplied reclaimed water

   C. Captured rainwater

   D. Wastewater from a toilet

   E. Graywater

Q7.8. Which of the following uses are best described and suitable
for nonpotable water? (Choose two)

   A. Drinking water

   B. Irrigation

   C. Clothes washing

   D. Process water

   E. Dishwashing

   F. Showers

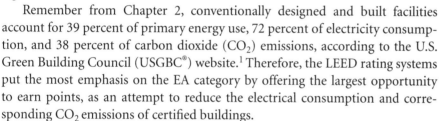

CHAPTER 8

ENERGY AND ATMOSPHERE

THIS CHAPTER FOCUSES ON THE STRATEGIES and technologies to address energy use and consumption as described in the Energy and Atmosphere (EA) category of the Leadership in Energy and Environmental Design (LEED®) rating systems. By now, we all understand the environmental impacts of using fossil fuels to generate electricity. Each step of the electricity production process harms the environment and ecosystem in one way or another. For example, the burning of coal releases harmful pollutants and greenhouse gases that contribute to global warming and climate change, reducing air quality on a global scale.

Remember from Chapter 2, conventionally designed and built facilities account for 39 percent of primary energy use, 72 percent of electricity consumption, and 38 percent of carbon dioxide (CO_2) emissions, according to the U.S. Green Building Council (USGBC®) website.[1] Therefore, the LEED rating systems put the most emphasis on the EA category by offering the largest opportunity to earn points, as an attempt to reduce the electrical consumption and corresponding CO_2 emissions of certified buildings.

Remember from Chapter 4, the EA category includes three prerequisites to set the minimum performance requirements to be achieved, thereby requiring any projects seeking certification to reduce demand at a minimum level. Beginning with an understanding of the requirements of these three prerequisites helps to comprehend the concepts of the EA category. These prerequisites are as follows:

- Fundamental Commissioning of Building Energy Systems
- Minimum Energy Performance
- Fundamental Refrigerant Management

COMMISSIONING

The first prerequisite of the EA category requires a new building to be commissioned by a commissioning agent (CxA). The commissioning process begins *early* in the design process in which the CxA works with the owner to establish the owner's project requirements (OPR). The OPR includes the environmental goals of the project and is issued to the design team to develop a basis of design (BOD) for the major building systems, such as lighting, domestic hot water, HVAC&R, and any renewable energy generated on-site. The commissioning process continues prior to the development of construction documents, as the CxA is required to review the design drawings and specifications to avoid

It's time to pick a different color for flashcards created for EA category topics.

TIP Burning coal releases the following harmful pollutants into the atmosphere: carbon dioxide, sulfur dioxide, nitrogen oxide, and mercury.

TIP Remember, it is best to assess and implement green building strategies as early as possible in the design process, including commissioning.

TIP HVAC&R stands for heating, ventilation, air conditioning, and refrigeration.

TIP The terms commissioning agent and commissioning authority can be used interchangeably.

Commissioning of new buildings has an average payback of 4.8 years and typically costs about $1 per square foot, according to a study conducted by Lawrence Berkley National Laboratory.[2]

 Retro-commissioning applies to the commissioning of existing buildings with an average simple payback of 0.7 years, according to a study conducted by Lawrence Berkley National Laboratory.[3]

 Create a flashcard to remember the benefits of a CxA:
1. Minimize or eliminate design flaws.
2. Avoid construction defects.
3. Avoid equipment malfunctions.
4. Ensure preventative maintenance is implemented during operations.

 Create a flashcard to remember ASHRAE 90.1-2007, Appendix L, as the baseline standard for energy performance.

 Any time you see ASHRAE 90.1, think ENERGY!

design flaws and ensure that the environmental goals are included, such as water and energy use reductions. The CxA works diligently during construction to ensure that the building system equipment is installed, calibrated, and performs appropriately and efficiently to avoid construction defects and equipment malfunctions. Before the building is occupied, the CxA helps to educate the facility management teams on the operation and maintenance strategies specific to the building. Within one year after occupancy, the CxA returns to the site to ensure that the building systems are working accordingly and address any needed adjustments.

MINIMUM ENERGY PERFORMANCE

Besides the Fundamental Commissioning prerequisite, the LEED rating systems also require buildings to perform to a minimum energy standard. Similar to the reference standard EPAct 1992 in the Water Efficiency (WE) category, which is used to create a baseline for comparison to the design case, a baseline is needed within the EA category to evaluate energy use reduction percentages of a project. Therefore, LEED references American Society of Heating, Refrigerating, and Air-Conditioning Engineers (ASHRAE) Standard 90.1-2007 to determine the minimum energy performance requirement for buildings seeking LEED certification.

The integrative design process is critical within all the LEED categories, but is essential within the EA category, especially when evaluating energy use (Figure 8.1). Energy performance, demands, and requirements are affected by multiple components, including:

■ Site conditions, such as heat island reduction, can reduce energy demand as equipment will not need to compensate for heat gain from surrounding and adjacent areas.

Figure 8.1 The Pennsylvania Department of Conservation and Natural Resources' Penn Nursery project incorporates radiant heat flooring to optimize its energy consumption. *Photo courtesy of Moshier Studio*

- Building orientation can affect the amount of energy needed for artificial heating, cooling, and lighting needs by taking advantage of passive design strategies, such as daylighting and natural ventilation.

- How much water needs to be heated or cooled? If building system equipment and fixtures require less water, less energy is therefore required. If all of the building equipment is sized appropriately and works efficiently, then less energy is demanded (Figures 8.2 and 8.3).

- Roof design can impact how much energy is required for heating and cooling by implementing a green roof or a roof with high solar reflective index (SRI) value.

 Minimize solar gain in the summer and maximize it in the winter with the help of passive design strategies! Passive designs capitalize on the four natural thermal processes: radiation, conduction, absorption, and convection.

 Remember, SRI is the acronym for solar reflective index and is synonymous with albedo. Do you remember the scale used for SRI? Is it better to have a higher or lower score?

Figure 8.2 High-efficiency boilers can help to achieve energy performance and savings goals. *Photo courtesy of SmithGroup, Inc.*

Figure 8.3 Installing high-efficiency chillers can help to achieve energy performance and savings goals. *Photo courtesy of SmithGroup, Inc.*

 TIP Building envelope refers to the system of walls, roofs, windows, and floor that form the exterior of a building.

- Building envelope thermal performance, including window selections, can reduce mechanical system sizing and energy demands by ensuring a thermal break between the interior and exterior environments.

- Light fixture types and the lamps/bulbs they require can reduce energy use by providing more light per square foot, but require fewer kilowatts per hour and therefore optimize **lighting power density.**

- Generating on-site renewable energy can reduce the amount of energy needed from the municipally supplied grid (Figure 8.4).

- Commissioning a building ensures that the equipment and systems are performing as they were intended, to maintain consistent and minimal energy demands.

- Educating occupants and operations and maintenance teams on how a building is intended to perform, what the environmental goals are, and providing them with the tools to monitor the performance will help to keep energy use to a minimum.

 TIP The key to energy modeling and simulation is whole-building evaluation, not individual component assessments. How do all of the systems work together?

The preceding bullet points describe the importance and need for project team members to work in a cohesive fashion to optimize the performance of a building and its site, ultimately reducing the amount of energy required for operations. Project teams are encouraged to take advantage of energy modeling and simulation software to study and evaluate how their specific project will function. Teams that utilize Building Information Modeling (BIM) software have an advantage to determine synergistic opportunities for their projects to add efficiencies. Both of these design phase studies also contribute to whole-building life-cycle cost assessments to determine trade-offs between up-front costs and long-term savings.

Figure 8.4 Installing wind turbines on-site helps to generate electricity needed for operations, reducing the demand from the grid. *Photo courtesy of Urban Green Energy*

Process Energy versus Regulated Energy

When a project team prepares and creates an energy simulation model (Figure 8.5), they should differentiate between **regulated** and **process energy**. LEED minimum energy performance criteria address only regulated energy, as process energy is not included or calculated. Regulated energy uses include the following:

 Create a flashcard to remember the uses of regulated energy.

- Lighting—interior and exterior applications (parking garages, facades, site lighting)

- HVAC—space heating, cooling, fans, pumps, toilet exhaust, ventilation for parking garages

- Service water for domestic and space heating purposes

Process energy uses include computers, office equipment, kitchen refrigeration and cooking, washing and drying machines, and elevators and escalators. Miscellaneous items, such as waterfall pumps and lighting that is exempt from lighting power allowance calculations such as lighting integrated into equipment,

 Create a flashcard to remember the uses of process energy.

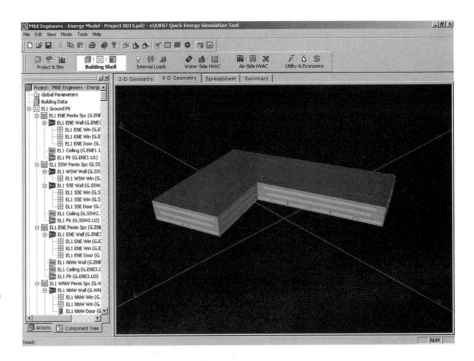

Figure 8.5 Modeling a proposed building can help project teams identify synergies to increase a building's performance and to calculate the energy saved based on those strategies. *Photo courtesy of M&E Engineers, Inc.*

are also categorized as process energy uses. For the purposes of the LEED Green Associate exam, it is important to remember the different process energy uses to understand what is included in the calculations for minimum and optimized energy performance requirements.

REFRIGERANTS

TIP Remember, chlorofluorocarbons (CFCs) are not allowed, and hydrochlorofluorocarbons (HCFCs) are to be phased out according to the Montreal Protocol.

Create a flashcard to remember that refrigerants should be evaluated based on ODP and GWP impacts and what these acronyms stand for.

TIP Existing Buildings: Operations & Maintenance (EBOM) projects must phase out CFC-based refrigerants in less than five years, leak less than 5 percent annually, and less than 30 percent over the remaining life.

TIP The Enhanced Refrigerant Management credit takes the requirements beyond the prerequisite to restrict the use of any refrigerants, as well as the use of **halons** for fire suppression systems. Halons, due to high ODP, have not been in production since they were banned in 1994 and are currently being phased out as required by the Montreal Protocol.

Besides commissioning and minimum energy performance prerequisites, the LEED rating systems also require buildings to manage refrigerants appropriately. Refrigerants enable the transfer of thermal energy and are therefore a critical component of air-conditioning and refrigeration equipment. Although they are cost effective, refrigerants have environmental trade-offs, as they contribute to ozone depletion and global warming. Therefore, project teams need to be mindful of the ozone-depleting potential (ODP) and global warming potential (GWP) of each refrigerant to determine the impact of the trade-offs, as an environmentally perfect refrigerant does not yet exist.

To comply with the Fundamental Refrigerant Management prerequisite, teams should refer to the Montreal Protocol when determining which refrigerants to use for their projects. The Montreal Protocol bans **chlorofluorocarbons** (CFCs) and requires **hydrochlorofluorocarbons** (HCFCs) to be phased out as they have the biggest impact on ozone depletion. CFC-based refrigerants are highest in ODP, more than HCFCs. Hydrofluorocarbon (HFC)-based refrigerants have no ODP but have GWP. Although other options exist that are not as harmful to the ozone, they have bigger and greater contributions to the production of greenhouse gases. These alternative options are also not as efficient as CFCs and HCFCs, and in turn, cause cooling systems to be less efficient by using more energy per unit of cooling output.

EXISTING BUILDINGS

As previously described, new construction and major renovation projects use ASHRAE 90.1-2007 as the baseline standard for energy performance. Existing buildings seeking LEED certification utilize a different resource, the Environmental Protection Agency's (EPA's) ENERGY STAR Portfolio Manager, as a benchmarking system for energy use (Figure 8.6). Portfolio Manager is a free online, web-based tool in which users enter electricity and natural gas consumption data to be evaluated against the performance of buildings with similar characteristics. Visit www.energystar.gov/index.cfm?c=evaluate_performance.bus_portfolio-manager for more information about the Portfolio Manager benchmarking tool.

For existing buildings where converting or replacing systems containing CFCs is not feasible, buildings must commit to phasing out the CFC-based refrigerants within five years from the end of the project's performance period. If the refrigerants are used in the central system, buildings must "reduce the annual leakage of CFC-based refrigerants to 5 percent or less and reduce the total leakage over the remaining life of the unit to less than 30 percent of its refrigerant charge, using **Clean Air Act**, Title VI, Rule 608 procedures governing refrigerant management and reporting."[4]

TIP An average ENERGY STAR rating from Portfolio Manager is 50, indicating the energy performance of a building.

Create a flashcard to remember that CFC refrigerants must be phased out within five years from the end of the performance period for EBOM projects.

TIP Remember, prerequisites are absolutely required, do not contribute to earning points, and ensure that certified buildings meet minimum performance criteria.

Figure 8.6 Facility managers and owners are encouraged to use the Environmental Protection Agency's (EPA's) ENERGY STAR Portfolio Manager tool to benchmark a building's performance. *Photo courtesy of U.S. EPA*

QUIZ TIME!

Q8.1. Which of the following are not subject to LEED minimum energy requirements? (Choose three)

A. Office equipment
B. Elevators
C. Chillers
D. Process energy
E. Regulated energy

Q8.2. When addressing refrigerants for a project and to comply with the Fundamental Refrigerant Management prerequisite, which of the following should be considered? (Choose three)

A. Fan motors and variable-frequency drives for ventilation air handlers
B. Base building air-conditioning systems
C. Boilers for heating systems
D. Reuse of existing HVAC&R systems
E. Elimination of substances with high ozone-depleting potential from use in air-conditioning and refrigeration systems

Q8.3. ASHRAE Standard 90.1-2007 is primarily concerned with which of the following? (Choose one)

A. Lighting design
B. Ventilation effectiveness

C. Energy consumption

D. Ozone depletion

Q8.4. Which of the following are categorized as regulated energy? (Choose three)

A. Computers

B. Space heating

C. Refrigeration

D. Service hot water

E. Lighting

Q8.5. Which of the following refrigerants is contained within fire suppression systems? (Choose one)

A. CFCs

B. HCFCs

C. HFCs

D. Chlorofluorocarbons

E. Halons

Q8.6. Which of the following are appropriate statements with regard to commissioning in the context of green building? (Choose two)

A. The CxA should be a primary member of the design team who is directly responsible for the project design or construction management.

B. The CxA should be separate and independent from those individuals who are directly responsible for project design or construction management (preferably from a separate firm).

C. The CxA is indirectly responsible for verifying the performance of building systems and equipment prior to installation, calibration, and operations.

D. The CxA is responsible for verifying the performance of building systems and equipment after installation.

STRATEGIES TO SATISFY EA PREREQUISITES AND CREDITS

 Create a flashcard to remember the four components of the EA category. Be sure to refer to Appendix D for a summary of all of the strategies to remember for the exam.

Project teams are encouraged to focus on the following four components in order to address the goals and intentions of the EA category to help reduce greenhouse gas emissions:

1. Energy Demand

2. Energy Efficiency

3. Renewable Energy

4. Ongoing Energy Performance

Energy Demand

The following five strategies, as listed in the *Green Building and LEED Core Concepts Guide*, address the energy demand of green buildings to help to save energy and therefore help to reduce greenhouse gas emissions and save money[5]:

1. *Establish design and energy goals.* Use standards such as ASHRAE 90.1 and California's Title 24, as well as benchmarks such as EPA's ENERGY STAR Portfolio Manager.

2. *Size the building appropriately.* Excessive and unnecessary vertical or horizontal square footage is wasteful and inefficient. Buildings should be designed to meet and not exceed the needs of the owner and occupants.

3. *Use free energy.* Natural resources should be explored early in the design process to meet the heating, cooling, ventilation, and lighting needs of a project (Figures 8.7, 8.8, and 8.9).

 Remember from the Study Tip listed in Chapter 4, LEED for Homes™ is the only rating system that addresses sizing a project appropriately using the Home Size Adjustment.

 Remember, adjacent buildings can be used as shade to help reduce cooling needs.

Figure 8.7 The Wetland Discovery Point building at Utah State University in Kaysville utilized a ground-source heat pump to exchange heating and cooling loads between the building and the earth to reduce their energy consumption by 30 percent. *Photo courtesy of Gary Neuenswander, Utah Agricultural Experiment Station*

Figure 8.8 Concord Hospital in Concord, New Hampshire, designed by Shepley Bulfinch, incorporates a green roof to optimize the energy performance of the building and skylights to allow daylighting to the interior environment, to further reduce the energy demand by reducing the need for artificial lighting. *Photo courtesy of Kat Nania, Shepley Bulfinch*

 Remember, green roofs help to insulate a building, therefore help to reduce energy demands. Can you name another benefit of a green roof?

 Remember the intentions of the SS and WE credits and prerequisites along with the requirements of the EA credits and prerequisites. Reducing water demands affects the SS, WE, and EA categories.

 Create a flashcard to remember the five strategies to address energy demand.

4. *Insulate* (Figure 8.10). High-performance building envelopes help to reduce the size of HVAC systems, thus help to use less energy.

5. *Monitor consumption* (Figure 8.11). For the same reasons metering is used as a strategy within the WE category, monitoring helps to ensure efficiency. Alarms and notifications can be set to alert staff of excess energy demands.

Energy Efficiency

Addressing the energy demands listed earlier is the first step of reducing required energy for building operations. Using energy efficiently builds off of the energy demand reduction strategies proposed and implemented. The goal to energy

Figure 8.9 The Wetland Discovery Point building at Utah State University utilizes a trombe wall to capture heat from the sun, as well as radiant heat flooring to increase the energy efficiencies of the project. *Photo courtesy of Gary Neuenswander, Utah Agricultural Experiment Station*

Figure 8.10 Spray foam insulation helps to seal any leaks of conditioned air to the exterior environment, therefore optimizing energy use. *Photo courtesy of BioBased Technologies*

Figure 8.11 Metering utilities to monitor consumption helps building owners and facility managers ensure that the building is functioning properly. *Photo courtesy of Gary Neuenswander, Utah Agricultural Experiment Station*

Create a flashcard to remember the units of measurement for energy: electricity is measured in kilowatts per hour, natural gas in therms, and liquid fuel in gallons.

Passive design strategies include maintaining a warm building in the winter, a cool building in the summer, and taking advantage of natural daylighting opportunities.

efficiency is to optimize **energy use intensity**, or to get the most out of a unit of energy. Energy use intensity is measured in **British thermal units (Btus) per square foot** or **kilowatt hours per square foot per year (kWh/sf/yr)**. Project teams assess the *energy use per square foot* when working with the majority of LEED rating systems and *use per capita* when working on a LEED for Neighborhood Development™ project.

Considering that the majority of a building's energy use is dedicated to space heating and lighting, addressing the efficiency for both is encouraged by the LEED rating systems. Evaluating the performance of the envelope and the efficiency of the building systems can reduce space-heating needs. When improving the efficiencies of lighting, project teams should tackle lighting strategies from a few different angles. First, the fixture type and count should be determined and calculated with the coordinating lamp or bulb type, with consideration for the use of each space. Remember, the goal is to meet the needs of the occupants, yet require minimal energy usage. For example, compact fluorescent lamps (CFLs) last longer and use less energy than conventional incandescent lamps, but deliver appropriate light levels. Using more energy, the incandescent fixtures emit more heat, in turn causing the mechanical system to work harder to cool a space. Finally, color schemes of interior spaces should also be considered when designing lighting plans. Lightly colored walls, workstations, and other interior elements tend to reflect more light than darker surfaces, allowing interior design decisions to stretch the efficiencies of light even further to possibly reduce the amount of required fixtures or lamps.

The *Green Building and LEED Core Concepts Guide* describes the following nine strategies to use energy more efficiently[6]:

1. *Identify passive design opportunities.* Take advantage of earth-supplied elements such as daylighting (Figures 8.12 and 8.13) and natural ventilation. Be mindful of orientation, building materials, and building envelope elements, such as window placement.

2. *Address the envelope.* Remember to incorporate high-performance glazing to avoid unwanted heat gain or loss, properly insulate the exterior walls and roof (Figure 8.14), and weatherize the building.

Figure 8.12 The sunshades at the Allegany County Human Resources Development Commission's community center in Cumberland, Maryland, depict one component of daylighting design strategies. Other possible components can include light shelves and window glazing to avoid glare. *Photo courtesy of Moshier Studio*

Patient Rooms ▲

Figure 8.13 This daylighting strategy at Concord Hospital helps to optimize natural light delivery to interior spaces to reduce the need for artificial lighting. *Image courtesy of Shepley Bulfinch*

Figure 8.14 Selecting insulated concrete forms (ICFs) as a building envelope material increases the energy performance of a building. *Photo courtesy of Moshier Studio*

Figure 8.15 Incorporating cooling towers can help to remove process waste heat by the means of water evaporation. *Photo courtesy of SmithGroup, Inc.*

3. *Install high-performance mechanical systems* (Figures 8.15 and 8.16). Determine the trade-offs of the up-front costs versus the operating costs by conducting a life-cycle cost analysis.

4. *Specify high-efficiency equipment and appliances.* Think ENERGY STAR for office equipment and appliances to reduce plug-load demands (Figure 8.17).

5. *Use high-efficient infrastructure for street lighting (Figure 8.18) and traffic signals.* Think about the consistent and long-term use of these fixtures to understand the value of longer life and cost savings from less energy required for operation.

6. *Capture efficiencies of scale* (Figure 8.19). Think about large universities or corporate campuses that use district systems to thermally condition multiple buildings on a single loop.

7. *Use thermal energy storage.* Refuse heat at night to provide cooling during the day in the summer and capture heat during the day to use at night in the winter (Figure 8.20).

8. *Use energy simulation.* Model the *whole building* with regulated energy uses to optimize synergies (Figure 8.21).

9. *Monitor and verify performance.* Commissioning, implementing building automation systems, and retro-commissioning all help to ensure energy efficiency.

 The environmental impacts of HVAC systems should be evaluated based on energy performance and the expected life of the equipment.

 Plug loads for typical American office buildings range from 0.5 to 1.00 watts per square foot.

 Ice generators use off-peak, cheaper energy to make ice at night used to cool the building during the day.

 Create a flashcard to remember the nine strategies to use energy more efficiently.

Figure 8.16 Utilizing a heat exchange system can help to reduce energy demands and save an owner operating costs. *Photo courtesy of SmithGroup, Inc.*

Figure 8.17 ENERGY STAR hot water heaters ensure efficiency. *Photo courtesy of Ashley Daigneault*

 Create a flashcard to remember the six types of qualifying renewable energy sources.

Renewable Energy

Keeping with the same goals previously discussed, implementing renewable energy technologies into a green building project can reduce the need to produce and consume coal, nuclear power, oil, and natural gases for energy, therefore reducing pollutants and emissions, as well as increasing air quality. For the purposes of LEED, eligible renewable energy sources include solar, wind, wave, biomass, geothermal power (Figure 8.22), and low-impact hydropower. The

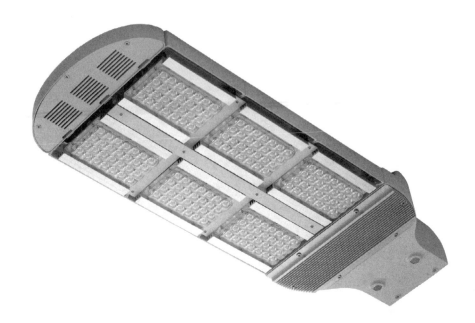

Figure 8.18 Installing light-emitting diode (LED) streetlight fixtures can help to decrease the energy demand for neighborhoods. *Photo courtesy of LED Waves*

Figure 8.19 The large hydroelectric generators at the Hoover Dam help to capture efficiencies of scale. *Photo courtesy of The Fischetti Family*

Green Building and LEED Core Concepts Guide describes the following two strategies to incorporate renewable energy and reduce the use of fossil fuels[7]:

1. *Generate on-site renewable energy.* Clean electricity must be generated on site by photovoltaic panels (Figure 8.23), wind turbines, geothermal, biomass, or low-impact hydropower. Think solar hot water heaters!

2. *Purchase green power or **renewable energy credits (RECs).*** Generated off site (Figure 8.24) and not associated with supplying power to a specific project site seeking LEED certification. Think tradable commodities!

TIP Building owners can purchase green power from a Green-e certified provider.

Create a flashcard to remember the meaning of the acronym REC. Create another flashcard to remember the two strategies to implement renewable energy into a green building project.

Figure 8.20 Ice ball thermal energy storage helps to provide cooling during the day from ice generated at night to reduce energy demands. *Photo courtesy of Cryogel*

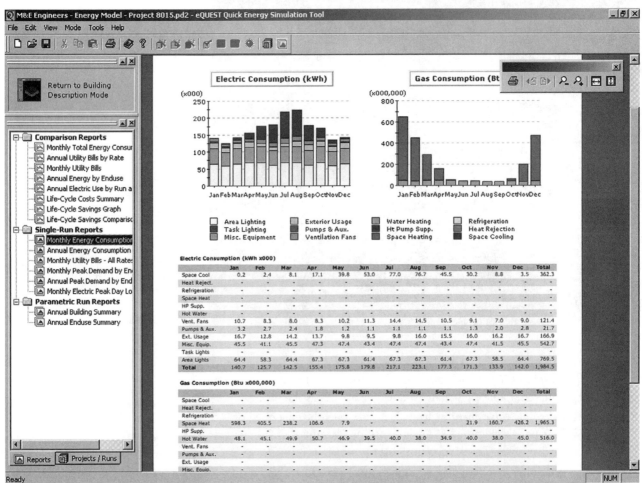

Figure 8.21 Energy modeling tools, such as eQUEST, assist project teams to determine energy consumptions. *Photo courtesy of M & E Engineers, Inc.*

Figure 8.22 Sherman Hospital in Elgin, Illinois, utilizes geothermal energy to minimize energy demands from the grid. *Photo courtesy of Shepley Bulfinch*

Figure 8.23 Stoller Vineyards in Dayton, Oregon, generates electricity on-site by the means of photovoltaic panels mounted on the roof. *Photo courtesy of Mike Haverkate, Stoller Vineyards*

Figure 8.24 Cedar Creek Wind Farm in Colorado helps to produce clean, renewable energy. *Photo courtesy of Brian Stanback, Renewable Choice Energy*

QUIZ TIME!

Q8.7. Which energy demand reduction strategies are missing from the list below? (Choose two)

Establish energy design and energy goals

Use free energy

Insulate

    A. Size the building appropriately

    B. Use thermal storage

    C. Monitor consumption

    D. Use energy simulation

    E. Purchase off-site renewable energy

Q8.8. Which of the following could contribute to earning the On-site Renewable Energy credit? (Choose three)

    A. Passive solar design concept that captures winter heat from the sun

    B. Photovoltaic panels that provide electricity to the building

    C. A wind farm located within 500 miles of the project and operated by the local utility company

    D. A ground-source heat pump that takes heat from the ground

    E. Solar hot water system

    F. An on-site electric generator powered by geothermal energy

    G. A solar farm adjacent to the project site providing clean power to the grid

Q8.9. What is the primary intent of the Green Power credit? (Choose one)

    A. To comply with the Montreal Protocol

    B. To encourage more solar farms in the United States and avoid carbon trading

    C. To encourage the development and use of renewable clean energy that is connected to the utility grid

    D. To minimize production of greenhouse gases by generating on-site renewable energy

Ongoing Energy Performance

The benefits of commissioning new buildings and retro-commissioning existing buildings include monitoring building system demands during operations. Tracking the performance of a green building ensures that the building operates as it was designed and intended. The *Green Building and LEED Core Concepts Guide* describes the following four strategies to ensure optimal performance[8]:

Figure 8.25 Inspecting building systems and educating the operations and maintenance staff on how the systems are intended to operate helps to ensure a building performs the way it was designed. *Photo courtesy of ENERActive Solutions*

1. *Adhere to the OPR.* Remember, this is the first part of the commissioning process that takes place as early as possible in the design process. This helps to communicate the environmental goals of the project to the design team, to be incorporated into the drawings and specifications.

2. *Provide staff training.* The building occupants should be aware of how to use less energy, such as turning off lights and computers after hours. Operations & maintenance staff should also be aware how to operate their facility and the way it was designed to function (Figure 8.25).

3. *Conduct preventative maintenance.* It typically costs less to be proactive than reactive. Scheduled maintenance keeps the building and its systems operating efficiently.

4. *Create incentives for occupants and tenants.* Provide feedback to occupants on energy usage to achieve and exceed the project's goals.

 Create a flashcard to remember the four ways to ensure optimal performance of a LEED-certified project.

 Project teams should follow four sequential steps to reduce energy use within their projects:
1. Reduce demand.
2. Employ means to use energy efficiently, such as high-performance equipment.
3. Assess renewable energy opportunities on and off site.
4. Monitor use to ensure that the building is operating and maintained accordingly.

QUIZ TIME!

Q8.10. Which of the following is not a measurement for energy use in the United States? (Choose one)

A. Kilowatt-hours for electricity

B. Liters for liquid fuel

C. Therms for natural gas

D. Gallons for liquid fuel

Q8.11. The engineer working on a new corporate building project seeking LEED for Core & Shell™ certification, has proposed a cogeneration system that provides electricity, cooling, heating, hot water, and dehumidification of outside air. The waste heat from the gas turbine–powered electric generator exhaust is designed and intended to drive an absorption chiller for cooling the building, therefore not using any CFCs or HCFCs. To which of the following LEED credits might these strategies contribute? (Choose two)

A. Commissioning

B. On-Site Renewable Energy

C. Enhanced Refrigerant Management

D. Green Power

E. Optimize Energy Performance

Q8.12. Which of the following *best* represents the typical range of plug loads for office buildings? (Choose one)

A. 0.1–0.25 watts per square foot

B. 0.5–1.00 watts per square foot

C. 20–30 watts per square foot

D. 5–10 watts per square foot

Q8.13. When should the OPR be prepared?

A. Schematic design

B. Construction documents

C. Design development

D. Beginning of construction

E. After substantial completion

CHAPTER **9**

MATERIALS AND RESOURCES

Figure 9.1 Specifying green materials, such as those with recycled content and that are locally extracted, processed, and manufactured, is a strategy to reduce the detrimental impacts of construction. *Photo courtesy of Skylar Nielson and 3-Form*

AS THE PREVIOUS CHAPTERS POINTED OUT, the built environment can be quite tolling on the natural environment. This book has so far presented means of minimizing impacts from the project site and reducing water and energy demands, while this chapter details strategies to minimize the environmental impacts of building materials as depicted in the Materials & Resources (MR) category in the Leadership in Energy and Environmental Design (LEED®) rating systems (Figure 9.1). This chapter details how to properly select materials and what to do with them after their useful life, two critical elements for the environment and the building industry, as buildings are a large consumer of natural resources. More specifically, a sustainability guide by San Mateo County suggests, "construction in the United States consumes 25 percent of all wood that is harvested, 40 percent of all raw stone, gravel and sand."[1] As a result, green building project team members are advised to evaluate the environmental impact of their materials and product specifications.

Project teams may then find themselves asking, "Where does steel come from? What kinds of materials are used to make green building products? How far did the raw material for the windows have to travel to the manufacturing plant? How far is the manufacturing plant from the project site? What happens to the leftover gypsum wallboard scraps?" To help answer these types of questions, this chapter addresses two components for consideration as related to material and resource selection and disposal:

1. The life-cycle impacts of building materials
2. Waste management during construction and operations

It's time to pick a different color for flashcards created for MR topics.

Create a flashcard to remember the two components to address within the MR category.

CONDUCTING LIFE-CYCLE ASSESSMENTS OF BUILDING MATERIALS TO DETERMINE SELECTIONS

Implementing sustainable building materials impacts a project's triple bottom line, just as with site selection and energy and water demands. As introduced in Chapter 2, project teams should perform **life-cycle assessments (LCAs)** of building materials, prior to specification, to evaluate the "cradle-to-grave" cycle of each material, especially as related to the environmental components of pollution and the demand of natural resources. The cradle-to-grave cycle includes the extraction location of raw materials, the manufacturing process and location, the impact on construction workers and building occupants, the expectancy term of use during operations, and the disposal options available. With the evaluation of these components, the results of an LCA will help to determine the material selections to include in the construction purchasing policy to help guide the contractor.

Although it may not be feasible to conduct a full LCA for every product, project teams can refer to the LEED reference guides for material selection assistance. The LEED rating systems suggest for project teams to implement products with one or more of the following characteristics, listed as follows and in Table 9.1:

■ Materials with **recycled content**—avoids landfills and incineration, reduces the need for virgin raw materials (Figure 9.2)

■ **Local/regional materials**—reduces transportation impacts, preserves local economy (Figure 9.3)

■ **Rapidly renewable materials**—preserves natural resource materials for future generations, can replace petroleum-based products

■ Forest Stewardship Council (FSC) **certified wood** materials—preserves materials for future generations and habitats and maintains biodiversity (Figure 9.4)

Table 9.1 Green Building Products

Characteristic		Description	Examples
Materials with recycled content		Products manufactured with material previously used	Masonry, concrete, carpet, acoustic ceiling tile, tile, rubber flooring, insulation, metal, and gypsum wallboard
	Preconsumer waste	Material left over from the manufacturing process	Fly ash, saw dust, walnut shells, sunflower seed hulls, obsolete inventories, and trimmings
	Postconsumer waste	Manufactured products at the end of their useful life	Any products that were consumed (such as metals, plastics, paper, cardboard, glass)
Local/regional materials		Products that are extracted, processed, and manufactured close to a project site	Materials obtained within 500 miles of the project site
Rapidly renewable materials		Animal or fiber materials that grow or can be raised in less than ten years	Bamboo flooring and plywood, cotton batt insulation, linoleum flooring, sunflower seed board panels, wheatboard cabinetry, wool carpeting, cork flooring, bio-based paints, geotextile fabrics, soy-based insulation, and straw bales
FSC certified wood materials		Sustainably managed forest resources	Contractors are required to show **chain-of-custody** (COC) documentation

 TIP Fly ash can be a substitution for Portland cement for concrete products. It is the residual component that is left behind during the coal incineration or combustion process.

 Create a flashcard to remember rapidly renewable fiber or animal materials must be grown or raised in ten years or less.

 Create a flashcard to remember the difference between preconsumer and postconsumer recycled contents.

 TIP ISO 14021-1999—Environmental Label and Declarations is the referenced standard that declares a material having postconsumer/preconsumer recycled content.

 Create a flashcard to remember the regional materials must be extracted, processed, *and* manufactured within 500 miles of the project site.

 Create a flashcard to remember that FSC wood requires chain-of-custody documentation.

Figure 9.2 Permeable pavers made with recycled content not only help to recharge the groundwater, but also help to reduce the need for virgin materials. *Photo courtesy of Vast Enterprises, LLC*

Figure 9.3 Purchasing materials that are extracted, processed, and manufactured within 500 miles helps to reduce the transportation impacts associated with building materials. *Photo courtesy of Gary Neuenswander, Utah Agricultural Experiment Station*

Figure 9.4 Purchasing wood from sustainable and responsible forests helps to ensure resources for future generations. *Photo courtesy of Gary Neuenswander, Utah Agricultural Experiment Station*

 Create a flashcard to remember the green building product characteristics and how they are calculated for LEED.

 Do you remember what form the contractor would fill in to upload to LEED-Online to show compliance with the recycled content, regional materials, certified wood, or rapidly renewable materials credits?

Calculating Green Building Products for LEED

The LEED rating systems award points to projects that surpass the minimum thresholds of green product purchasing and therefore the products are required to be tracked, measured, and calculated to prove compliance. Materials with recycled content, regional materials, salvaged materials, and rapidly renewable animal or fiber products are calculated as a percentage of the total material cost for a project. FSC wood products are calculated as a percentage of the total cost of new wood products purchased for a specific project. After construction, materials are then documented and tallied to show compliance to earn points. For example, should a project purchase 60 percent of their wood products from a sustainably managed forest, they would earn one point, as the minimum threshold is to purchase at least

50 percent FSC certified wood of total wood purchased. If only portions of assembled products or materials can contribute to earning the credit, those portions are calculated as a percentage of weight of the cost of the assembled item. For example, if only 80 percent (by weight) of a carpet system has recycled content, only 80 percent of the material cost can contribute toward earning the Recycled Content credit.

QUIZ TIME!

Q9.1. Which of the following materials could contribute to earning the Recycled Content credit, as preconsumer recycled content? (Choose three)

A. Metal stud manufacturing scrap sent back into the same manufacturing process

B. Paper towels manufactured from cardboard used for packaging

C. Medium-density fiberboard panels manufactured with sawdust generated by the manufacturing of structural insulated panels

D. Concrete made with fly ash collected from coal-burning power plants

E. Carpet padding manufactured with waste fiber collected from textile manufacturing plants

Q9.2. The percentage calculation for rapidly renewable materials accounts for which of the following? (Choose two)

A. Cost of rapidly renewable materials

B. Volume of rapidly renewable materials

C. Combined weight for all rapidly renewable materials

D. Total materials cost for the project

Q9.3. Which of the following is not an example of rapidly renewable materials? (Choose one)

A. Strawboard

B. Oak wood flooring

C. Cotton insulation

D. Cork flooring

E. Wheatboard

BUILDING MATERIAL LIFE-CYCLE IMPACTS

The LEED rating systems not only help to define the parameters of green building products, but also help to identify environmentally responsible procurement strategies during both construction and operations, as the first strategy to reduce the life-cycle impacts of the products used at a project site. As previously mentioned, architects need to specify materials appropriately to provide contractors the guidelines for the types of building materials they should purchase and use during construction. During operations, building owners and facility managers should address the products they are purchasing by also implementing sustainable procurement policies. As the LEED for Existing Buildings: Operations + Maintenance™ (EBOM) rating system dictates, these policies can address the goals and thresholds for purchasing ongoing consumables, such as lamp types, food, cleaning products, and paper products; and durable goods, such as electronics and furniture.

Although LEED EBOM is the only rating system that includes a sustainable purchasing policy *prerequisite*, each of the rating systems offer other opportunities to earn points for projects that implement similar policies. In addition to sustainable purchasing, projects can also implement the following strategies to reduce the impacts of materials and products on the environment[2]:

▲ **Figure 9.5** Sustainable procurement choices, such as cradle-to-cradle (C2C) certified task chairs composed of recycled content, helps to avoid landfills and the need for virgin materials. *Photo courtesy of Steelcase, Inc.*

▶ **Figure 9.6** Specifying cradle-to-cradle (C2C) certified surfaces made of recycled content with low to no volatile organic compounds (VOCs) helps to reduce the need of virgin materials, as well as, improve the indoor environment. *Photo courtesy of Icestone, LLC, and Green Team*

1. *Specify green materials.* Can you name the four types previously discussed in this chapter? Figures 9.5 and 9.6 will provide a hint of one type.

2. *Specify green interiors.* Keep volatile organic compounds (VOCs) to a minimum (Figures 9.6, 9.7, and 9.8). See Chapter 10 for more information.

3. *Specify green electronic equipment.* Remember ENERGY STAR equipment and appliances from the EA category? BEES, the construction carbon calculator, ECOCalculator for assemblies, and EPEAT offer LCAs to help select equipment that use energy efficiently, are made with recyclable and recycled materials, and tend to require less maintenance and are upgradable.

 TIP BEES = Building for Environmental and Economic Sustainability, www.wbdg.org/tools/bees.php

EPEAT = Electronic Product Environmental Assessment Tool, www.epeat.net

 Create a flashcard to remember the three strategies to address the impacts of building material selection and procurement.

Figure 9.7 Installing CRI Green Label Plus Program carpet tiles avoids the contamination of the indoor air. *Photo courtesy of Beaulieu Commercial*

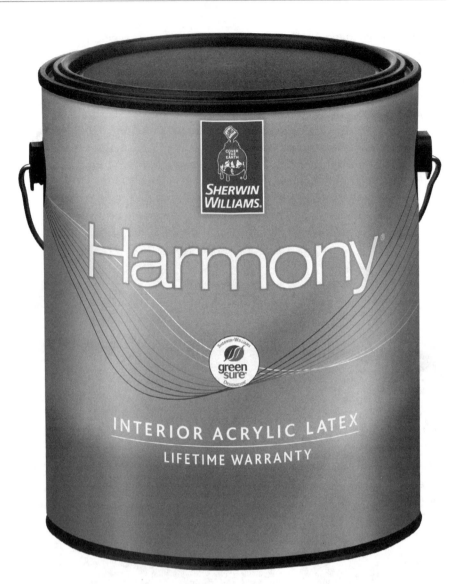

Figure 9.8 Specifying low-VOC paint not only provides a better indoor environment for the occupants, but a safer work environment for construction workers. *Photo courtesy of Sherwin-Williams*

QUIZ TIME!

Q9.4. A library is to be constructed with wood posts and beams salvaged from barns in the region, and purchased FSC Certified Wood for doors and trim. The owner is interested in determining whether the project meets the requirements of certified wood for LEED. The qualification of products and determination of their contribution to certified wood requires keeping track of which of the following? (Choose two)

A. Cost of certified wood products as a percentage of the total material cost of the project

B. Cost of certified wood products as a percentage of the total cost for wood products purchased for the project

C. Weight of certified wood products as a percentage of all new wood products used on the project

D. Chain-of-custody documentation for all FSC certified wood products

E. Chain-of-custody documentation for all new wood products purchased for the project

Q9.5. Which of the following resources should a facility manager consult in reference to finding more information about sustainable purchasing options? (Choose three)

A. EPAT

B. ENERGY STAR Portfolio Manager

C. ENERGY STAR

D. EPA

E. BEES

WASTE MANAGEMENT

Construction processes and building operations should be addressed to minimize environmental impacts from disposal and waste. In the United States, building construction and demolition alone account for 40 percent of the total waste stream, while building operations account for 300 tons of waste per year for a building with 1,500 employees.[3]

 Landfills require sunlight, moisture, and oxygen in order to decompose material; quite a challenging feat for a dark, enclosed environment, don't you think?

When waste is collected and hauled from a construction site or an existing facility, it is typically brought to a landfill or an incineration facility, both of which contribute to greenhouse gas emissions. Landfills produce and then leak methane and incineration facilities processes produce carbon dioxide. As another environmental detriment, think about the potential for landfills to contaminate groundwater sources. As a result, green building project teams and facility managers are encouraged to address **waste diversion** strategies for new and existing buildings to avoid landfills and incineration facilities.

The EPA estimates a reduction of 5 million metric tons of carbon dioxide, if recycling efforts were to increase just 3 percent above the current 32 percent rate.[4] To help reach this goal, the LEED rating systems offer point opportunities for implementing waste management policies during construction, to divert waste by reuse and recycling strategies. Construction waste management plans should address whether waste will be separated on-site into individually labeled waste containers or collected in a **commingled** fashion in one container and sorted off-site (Figure 9.9). As with many of the components addressed within the LEED rating systems, there are trade-offs to address when deciding between the two options. Commingled collection reduces the amount of space needed on-site, while on-site collection may require additional labor to manage the sorting effort. In either case, land clearing debris and soil should not be included in the calculations, but metals, concrete, and asphalt should all be collected for recycling and accounted for (Figure 9.10). Recycling options for paper, cardboard, plastics, and wood varies by region.

 Create a flashcard to remember the EPA statistic for current recycling rates of 32 percent.

 Create a flashcard to remember the minimum types of items to be recycled during operations to meet the requirements of the MR prerequisite: paper, corrugated cardboard, glass, plastics, and metals.

Each of the rating systems includes a prerequisite to address waste management policies during operations for the collection and storage of recyclables. At a minimum, LEED projects must recycle paper, corrugated cardboard, glass, plastics, and metals. LEED EBOM offers point opportunities for auditing waste streams and implementing waste management policies for

 Do you remember the two prerequisites from the MR category for LEED EBOM projects?

 Create a flashcard to remember the 3Rs of waste management: Reduce, Reuse, and Recycle. Remember them in that order as a hierarchal approach for policies.

▶ **Figure 9.9** Separating waste on site is one method to comply with the Construction Waste Management strategies to avoid landfills and incineration facilities. *Photo courtesy of Auld & White Constructors, LLC*

▼ **Figure 9.10** Dedicated waste container for masonry to be collected for recycling.

ongoing consumables (such as soap, batteries, and paper goods) and durable goods (such as furniture and electronics). Think about the potential for air and water contamination from batteries and fluorescent light bulbs, if they were not recycled.

Strategies to Reduce Waste[5]

1. *Size the building appropriately.* Can you remember the rating systems that address this strategy? Smaller buildings use less energy and have lower operating costs.

2. *Develop a construction waste management policy.* Goals addressed as a 50 percent diversion could earn a point by reducing, reusing, or recycling.

3. *Encourage recycling.* The storage and collection of recyclables is required for projects seeking LEED certification (Figure 9.11).

4. ***Reuse or salvage*** *building materials.* Extends useful life of products and reduces the need for raw materials (Figure 9.12). Also can save money as opposed to buying new.

5. *Reuse existing buildings* instead of tearing down and building new (Figure 9.13).

6. *Compost.* Use landscaping and food debris as mulch (Figure 9.14).

7. *Consider new technology, design, and construction decisions.* Consider finishing concrete floors (Figure 9.15) to avoid the need for a floor finish such as carpet or ceramic tile, or consider specifying carpet tiles (Figure 9.16) in lieu of roll goods to minimize the amount needed for replacement should an area get damaged.

  TIP Waste is calculated in volume or weight (tons).

TIP Salvaged materials are calculated as a percentage of total material cost of a project. What other types of green building materials are calculated this way? Which ones are calculated as a percentage of the total material volume or weight?

 Do you remember the benefits of mulching discussed in Chapter 7?

 Create a flashcard to remember the seven strategies to reduce waste.

Figure 9.11 Recycling during operations is required of all projects seeking LEED certification. *Photo courtesy of Jason Hagopian, AIA, LEED AP*

▲ **Figure 9.12** The ebony oak wood for the reception desk and other areas at One Haworth Center in Holland, Michigan, was recovered from the Great Lakes and other waterways to avoid depleting old-growth forests. *Photo courtesy of Haworth Inc.*

▶ **Figure 9.13** Finding new uses for existing buildings helps to extend the life of the existing building stock and avoids demolition and waste. *Photo courtesy of SmithGroup, Inc.*

Figure 9.14 Using a compost bin to dispose of food and landscaping debris helps to generate mulch to use on-site for landscaping. *Photo courtesy of the Fischetti Family*

Figure 9.15 Finishing concrete floors eliminates the need for additional finishes and therefore helps to preserve resources. *Photo courtesy of L&M Construction Chemicals, Inc.*

Figure 9.16 Installing carpet tiles in lieu of roll goods saves on operational costs for replacement. *Photo courtesy of Beaulieu Commercial*

QUIZ TIME!

Q9.6. Which of the following greenhouse gases is a by-product of landfills? (Choose one)

A. Carbon monoxide

B. Methane

C. Sulfur dioxide

D. Nitrous oxide

Q9.7. Which of the following statements are not true about green building materials? (Choose two)

A. Rapidly renewable materials are harvested within ten years.

B. Cradle-to-grave materials can be recycled.

C. Products with postconsumer recycled content can contribute to earning the Recycled Content LEED credit while products with preconsumer recycled content cannot.

D. Cotton insulation can be considered a type of rapidly renewable material.

Q9.8. Which of the following would the contractor upload to LEED-Online? (Choose two)

A. Stormwater management plan

B. Total amount of waste diverted from a landfill

C. The total material cost of the project and the percentage containing recycled content

D. Energy modeling calculations to show expected energy savings

Q9.9. When addressing materials and resources, a project team should incorporate which of the following to comply with the credits and prerequisites of the MR category within the LEED rating systems? (Choose three)

A. The purchasing policy of the manufacturer

B. Location of manufacturing plant of steel

C. The type of car the CEO drives

D. Postconsumer recycled content of a chair

E. Extraction location of silica

Q9.10. How would a contractor show proof of compliance for FSC certified wood for a LEED NC project? (Choose one)

A. Give the architect a spreadsheet summarizing all of the wood was purchased with 500 miles of the project site.

B. Upload receipts of FSC wood purchased to LEED-Online.

C. Upload chain-of-custody documentation to LEED-Online.

D. Complete a credit submittal template and upload it to LEED-Online including the chain-of-custody numbers and invoice amounts.

E. Mail all documentation to USGBC.

Q9.11. Which of the following is not considered an ongoing consumable product? (Choose one)

A. Soap

B. Batteries

C. Furniture

D. Paper towels

E. Lamp bulbs

Q9.12. How is waste hauled from a construction site calculated for the purposes of LEED? (Choose one)

A. As a percentage of total material cost of a project

B. As a percentage of the total material volume or weight

C. As a percentage of total cost of a project

D. In tons

CHAPTER **10**

INDOOR ENVIRONMENTAL QUALITY

THIS CHAPTER FOCUSES ON THE ELEMENTS INVOLVED to improve the indoor environment as detailed in the Indoor Environmental Quality (IEQ) category of the Leadership in Energy and Environmental Design (LEED®) rating systems. Remember that Chapter 2 introduced the importance of indoor environments, since Americans typically spend about 90 percent of their time indoors, according to the Environmental Protection Agency (EPA). The EPA also

Figure 10.1 Addressing such factors as daylighting, views, and low-emitting material selections helps to bring value to the indoor environmental quality. *Photo courtesy of Haworth Inc.*

It's time to pick a different color for flashcards created for Indoor Environmental Quality topics.

Create a flashcard to remember the four components of the IEQ category.

Increasing ventilation may improve the overall IAQ, but it may increase the energy demand of heating, ventilation, and air conditioning (HVAC) systems at the same time.

reports conventionally designed, constructed, and maintained indoor environments have significantly higher levels of pollutants than the outdoors.[1] However, studies have shown that green buildings with improved interior environmental quality "have the potential to enhance the lives of building occupants, increase their resale value of the building, and reduce the liability for building owners."[2] Because employee salaries and benefits are the biggest cost for a business, larger than operating costs for facilities, such as utilities, the satisfaction and health of the occupants should be a high priority. Retaining employees in order to avoid the additional costs of training new hires can help to add efficiencies to the economic bottom line for businesses. Reducing absenteeism due to health impacts increases productivity and reduces liability of inadequate indoor environmental quality. Businesses, such as Haworth, will enjoy a return on their investment for increasing their employee satisfaction by providing a comfortable work environment (Figure 10.1). The LEED rating systems offer the following strategies to improve indoor environments:

1. Indoor Air Quality
2. Thermal Comfort
3. Lighting
4. Acoustics

INDOOR AIR QUALITY

The *LEED Reference Guide for Building Design and Construction* (BD+C) uses the American Society of Heating, Refrigerating, and Air-Conditioning Engineers' (ASHRAE's) definition for **indoor air quality** (IAQ) as it states "the nature of air inside the space that affects the health and well-being of building occupants."[3] Studies have shown that poor indoor air quality can lead to respiratory disease, allergies and asthma, and **sick building syndrome**, and can therefore impact the performance and productivity of employees. The LEED rating systems address components from a triple bottom line perspective, to improve air quality during construction and operations to avoid effects on human health and to improve the quality of life.

IAQ During Construction

During construction, project teams should follow the practices recommended by the **Sheet Metal and Air Conditioning Contractors' National Association (SMACNA)** guidelines. Contractors need to be mindful of reducing or eliminating contaminants from entering the indoor environment, including mechanical systems, to deliver an environment with better air quality. Contaminants include **volatile organic compounds (VOCs)**, carbon dioxide, particulates, and tobacco smoke. SMACNA guidelines recommend VOCs from furniture, paints, adhesives, and carpets should be kept below defined maximum levels to avoid polluting the indoor environment (Figure 10.2). For the purposes of LEED, the indoor environment to be protected from high levels of VOCs includes any spaces where products and materials are applied on-site and within the weatherproofing system.

Figure 10.2 Specifying materials with low to no VOCs helps to maintain good indoor air quality. *Photo courtesy of Sherwin-Williams*

Industry standards, such as Green Seal (for paints, coatings, adhesives, etc.), South Coast Air Quality Management District (SCAQMD) (for sealants), the Carpet and Rug Institute (CRI), and Floorscore specify the maximum levels of VOCs, in grams per liter (g/L), not to be exceeded. Other standards, such as Greenguard™ and Scientific Certification Systems (SCS) Indoor Advantage, certify products, such as furniture, that do not off-gas harmful levels of pollutants.

Composite wood and agrifiber products may also off-gas and therefore should be evaluated for inclusion for green building interior construction. The *LEED Building Design and Construction (BD+C)* reference guide defines composite wood and agrifiber products as "particleboard, medium-density fiberboard (MDF), plywood, wheatboard, strawboard, panel substrates and door cores."[4] These products, also including oriented strand board (OSB), are manufactured with resin products to bind the fibers to hold the products together and form the useful material. To comply within the parameters of LEED, composite wood and agrifiber products cannot contain any added **urea-formaldehyde** resins, which off-gas at room temperature, to avoid contaminating the interior environment and therefore avoid causing health problems. Although many exterior building

Create a flashcard to remember what VOCs are, the different referenced standards, the types of VOCs, and that they are measured in g/L.

Create a flashcard to remember that urea-formaldehyde is not allowed, but pheno-formaldehyde is suitable.

Create a flashcard to remember MERV and 1–16 range of filters.

products may contain **pheno-formaldehyde**, this resin only off-gases at high temperatures, and is therefore allowed within the confines of LEED compliance.

The SMACNA guidelines also address ventilation as a means to maintain quality indoor air, as well as the requirements for filtration media at all air returns (Figure 10.3). The LEED rating systems follow suit with SMACNA practices and therefore, also recommend employing **Minimum Efficiency Reporting Value (MERV) filters** to ensure effectiveness. The rating of MERV filters ranges from 1 (low) to 16 (highest), where LEED requires a minimum of MERV 8 filters (Figure 10.4) to be implemented at return air intake locations for compliance. Before occupancy, LEED recommends air quality testing to ensure nonharmful air levels for occupants or conducting a building flush-out to eliminate any pollutants in the air caused by construction processes and activities. A building flush-out requires the mechanical system to be flushed out with outside air to remove residual contaminants.

The SMACNA construction manual also recommends good housekeeping practices during construction, to protect absorptive materials from moisture damage to later prevent the growth of toxic substances, such as mold. These materials, such as drywall, acoustical ceiling tiles, and carpet, should be stored in dry, elevated (Figure 10.5), and protected areas to avoid coming into contact with liquids.

IAQ During Operations

TIP CO_2 concentrations greater than 530 parts per million (ppm) as compared to exterior environments are typically harmful to occupants.

During building operations, indoor air pollutants should also be monitored to continue to reduce impacts on occupants. Incorporating green cleaning products with low or no VOCs helps to reduce pollutants and contaminants from entering the indoor airflow. Also, MERV filters should be changed regularly and carbon dioxide levels should be monitored to help ensure good air quality. Maintenance strategies should also employ low or no VOC products, such as paints

Figure 10.3 SMACNA-compliant practices include sealing off ductwork from dust and particulates.

Figure 10.4 Installing MERV 8 filters or better will help to improve the indoor air quality by eliminating dust and particles. *Photo courtesy of Auld & White Constructors, LLC*

Figure 10.5 Elevated product storage for protection against damage as suggested by SMACNA guidelines.

and adhesives. Integrated pest management strategies avoid the use of pesticides to eliminate human exposure; nonchemical monitor and bait strategies should be implemented instead.

Project teams and facility managers are encouraged to design for and provide adequate ventilation for occupants without compromising energy use efficiencies, not to be a burden on the environment by contributing to the need for

Figure 10.6 Installing operable windows provides building occupants access to means of adequate ventilation. *Photo courtesy of Gary Neuenswander, Utah Agricultural Experiment Station*

 TIP Any time you see ASHRAE 62, think IAQ! Say it out loud: IAQ 62, 62 IAQ!

fossil fuels. Mechanical systems should work to thermally balance outdoor air with every air change; therefore, the key is to find the right balance. Too many air changes are wasteful and would impact economic and environmental bottom lines. However, too little ventilation can result in reduced quality of the indoor air, which would impact the health and satisfaction of occupants, thus also affecting the triple bottom line components. Therefore, project teams designing green buildings use the industry standard, **ASHRAE 62.1, Ventilation for Acceptable Indoor Air Quality**, to adequately and appropriately size mechanical systems that will deliver the proper amounts of outside air while balancing energy demands. ASHRAE 62 describes proper **ventilation rates**, or the "amount of air circulated through a space, measured in air changes per hour."[5]

Strategies

The *Green Building and LEED Core Concepts Guide* suggests nine strategies to address indoor air quality[6]:

1. *Prohibit smoking.* Not only indoors, but also be aware of mechanical system contamination at all air intakes and operable windows (Figure 10.6). Designate smoking areas to avoid affecting building occupants.

2. *Ensure adequate ventilation.* Think ASHRAE 62!

3. *Monitor carbon dioxide.* Incorporate **demand-controlled ventilation** where airflow is increased if maximum set points are exceeded.

4. *Install high-efficiency air filters.* Remember MERV!

5. *Specify low-emitting materials.* For interior finishes, such as paints, carpet, and furniture. Remember industry standards such as Green Seal, SCAQMD, CRI, Floorscore, SCS Indoor Advantage, and Greenguard™ (Figure 10.7).

6. *Use integrated pest management.* To eliminate contaminants indoors, no pesticides should enter the facility.

7. *Protect air quality during construction.* Remember SMACNA practices.

Figure 10.7 Specifying Greenguard™-certified furniture helps to maintain quality indoor air. *Photo courtesy of Steelcase, Inc.*

Figure 10.8 Requiring the use of green cleaning products will ensure that no harmful chemicals are used to contaminate the air. *Photo courtesy of Absolute Green*

8. *Conduct a flush-out.* Opening the windows is not enough to remove construction pollutants! Ductwork should be flushed out with a large amount of outside air.

9. *Employ a green cleaning program.* No harmful chemicals (Figure 10.8)! Equipment should follow environmental standards and requirements for optimized use.

 Create a flashcard to remember the nine strategies of IAQ. Remember, Appendix D summarizes all of the strategies to remember.

QUIZ TIME!

Q10.1. Which of the following is consistent with the range of MERV filter ratings? (Choose one)

  A. 1–30
  B. 0–50
  C. 1–110
  D. 1–16
  E. 1–100

Q10.2. Which of the following are consistent with the requirements of Low-Emitting Materials: Adhesives & Sealants? (Choose three)

  A. All adhesives and sealants must not exceed the VOC limits set by ASHRAE 232-1998: Maximum VOC Emissions in Occupied Spaces with Recirculating Air.

  B. Nonaerosol adhesives and sealants must be in compliance with VOC limits set by SCAQMD, Rule 1168.

  C. Paints and coatings must contain no phenol-formaldehyde.

  D. Adhesives and sealants must carry a Green Spec seal of approval.

E. Aerosol adhesives must meet VOC limits established by the Green Seal Standard (GS-36).

F. While projects are encouraged, but not required, to use low-VOC adhesives and sealants on exterior building elements, all adhesives and sealants inside of the building envelope weather seal must meet the requirements of the referenced standards.

Q10.3. Which of the following are standards for indoor air quality? (Choose three)

A. Greenguard™

B. ASHRAE 90.1

C. CRI Green Label Plus

D. Green Seal

E. ENERGY STAR

Q10.4. SCAQMD Rule 1168 refers to which of the following? (Choose one)

A. Measures air-change effectiveness

B. Describes ventilation requirements for acceptable indoor air quality

C. Defines the use of urea- and phenol-formaldehyde in composite wood and agrifiber products

D. Sets the VOC maximum content for adhesives and sealants

E. Sets the VOC maximum content for paints and coatings

F. Defines the maximum allowable VOC emissions for carpets and carpet cushions

Q10.5. Which of the following statements is not a strategy to maintain indoor air quality? (Choose one)

A. Open all windows to flush contaminated air out of a building for at least two weeks prior to occupancy.

B. Coordinate a green cleaning program.

C. Install high-efficiency filters.

D. Specify adhesives and sealants with low or no VOCs.

THERMAL COMFORT

TIP Anytime you see ASHRAE 55, think *thermal comfort*. What do you think of when you see ASHRAE 90.1? How about ASHRAE 62?

Create a flashcard to remember the three environmental factors of thermal comfort defined by ASHRAE 55.

The *Green Building and LEED Core Concepts Guide* defines thermal comfort as "the temperature, humidity, and airflow ranges within which the majority of people are most comfortable, as determined by **ASHRAE Standard 55-2004**."[7] ASHRAE 55 indicates the three environmental factors that impact thermal comfort: humidity, air speed, and temperature. Although temperature settings should vary with the seasons, buildings should allow for occupants to control their thermal conditions to optimize satisfaction and comfort. Remember, occupants who are satisfied and comfortable tend to be more productive! For the purposes of LEED, occupants must be able to control one of the three components of thermal comfort.

Strategies

The *Green Building and LEED Core Concepts Guide* describes three strategies to offer thermal comfort to occupants[8]:

Create a flashcard to remember the three strategies for thermal comfort.

1. *Install operable windows* for fresh air access (Figure 10.9).
2. *Give occupants temperature and ventilation control.* If operable windows are not feasible, give occupants control over mechanically supplied and delivered warm or cool air by employing strategies such as raised access floors (Figure 10.10).
3. *Conduct occupant surveys.* Discover the overall satisfaction of the thermal comfort levels of the majority of the occupants to determine areas for improvement.

Figure 10.9 Wausau's LEED Silver facility in Wausau, Wisconsin, employs operable windows to give their employees access to fresh air. *Photo courtesy of Wausau Windows and Wall Systems*

Figure 10.10 Raised access floors provide the flexibility to grant occupants individual control of the amount of air supplied through diffusers for their thermal comfort. *Photo courtesy of Tate Access Floors, Inc.*

QUIZ TIME!

Q10.6. When addressing thermal comfort, which of the following are not addressed? (Choose two)

   A. Humidity

   B. Ventilation requirements

   C. Air movement

   D. Artificial light

   E. Average temperature

Q10.7. An environmental tobacco smoke control policy *best* addresses which of the following? (Choose one)

   A. Providing ventilation requirements to effectively remove tobacco smoke

   B. Providing dedicated smoking rooms 25 feet away from building entrances

   C. Preventing tobacco smoke from contaminating indoor environments

   D. Preventing tobacco smoke from entering the air occupied by nonsmokers

TIP A study found students in daylit classrooms progressed 20 percent faster in math and 26 percent faster in reading as compared to students studying in artificially lit classrooms.[9]

LIGHTING

The LEED rating systems address lighting in terms of naturally available daylight and artificially supplied light. When debating whether to incorporate daylighting strategies, project teams are advised to conduct a life-cycle cost analysis to determine the up-front costs and operational savings. For example, when using daylighting strategies, sensors could be installed to trigger alternative light sources when needed, which would impact up-front costs, although the costs can be offset by the energy saved during operations since less artificial light would be required. Daylighting can also result in improved occupant satisfaction and health due to access and connection to the exterior environment, also affecting the economic bottom line over time (Figure 10.11).

Besides daylighting, providing occupants with the ability to control their lighting needs can also benefit the triple bottom line. Occupant-controlled lighting contributes to employee satisfaction, as well as productivity, as light levels can be altered for specific tasks, needs, and preferences (Figure 10.12). Therefore, providing

When one is designing, nonregularly occupied spaces should be placed at the core to allow offices, classrooms, and other regularly occupied areas to be placed along the window line.

Remember, building orientation and passive design strategies impact the opportunities to utilize daylighting to supply ambient lighting for occupants.

Figure 10.11 A classroom at Northland Pines High School in Eagle River, Wisconsin, provides students and teachers accessibility to views of the outdoor environment, as well as daylighting to improve their satisfaction and productivity. *Photo courtesy of Hoffman, LLC*

Figure 10.12 Providing occupants with task lighting allows for more individual control of work environments to improve their satisfaction and productivity. *Photo courtesy of Skylar Nielson, 3form*

Figure 10.13 Providing interior environments with access to natural daylight not only improves the occupants' satisfaction and productivity levels, but also helps to reduce the need for artificial lighting to reduce operating costs. *Photo courtesy of Steelcase, Inc.*

TIP Project teams should design the overall illumination light level to be about 40 to 60 footcandles on an office work surface.

Create a flashcard to remember the three strategies to improve lighting in reference to IEQ.

overall ambient light, as well as individual task lighting, is the best strategy to address lighting needs. Facilities can also see a reduction in energy usage for lighting needs by educating employees on the benefits of turning off fixtures after use.

Strategies

The *Green Building and LEED Core Concepts Guide* suggests the following strategies to address lighting for a green building project[10]:

1. *Use daylighting.* Remember passive design strategies and benefits (Figure 10.13).
2. *Give occupants lighting control* for economic benefits from energy savings while improving occupant satisfaction.
3. *Conduct occupant surveys.* Discover the overall satisfaction of the lighting levels of the majority of the occupants to determine areas for improvement.

QUIZ TIME!

Q10.8. Which of the following is the labeling standard applicable to carpets and carpet pads? (Choose two)

    A. CRI Green Label+

    B. Green-e

    C. Green carpets

    D. Green Seal

    E. Green Seal 36

    F. CRI Green Label

Q10.9. A 60,000-square-foot existing timber frame building is undergoing a major renovation, including the addition of 140,000 more square feet. This 200,000-square-foot renovation project reuses the existing structure, replaces single-pane windows with energy-efficient glazing manufactured in a nearby town, and installs salvaged wood floors donated from an adjacent property. Which of the following credits may be applicable to this project's LEED certification application? (Choose two)

A. Certified Wood

B. Low-Emitting Materials: Composite Wood & Agrifiber

C. Optimize Energy Performance

D. Local/Regional Materials

E. Construction Waste Management

Q10.10. Which of the following best describes the LEED strategy applicable to ASHRAE Standard 62.1-2007? (Choose one)

A. Exterior lighting levels

B. Thermal comfort by means of controllability of systems

C. Environmental tobacco smoke control

D. Ventilation and indoor air quality

E. Building flush-out parameters and guidelines

ACOUSTICS

For those who have worked in an open plan office environment, there is an appreciation for attention to proper acoustic design components. The ability to communicate effectively, in person or via telecommunications, is impacted by the quality of acoustics. For educational environments, the LEED for Schools™ rating system addresses high-performance acoustic design for core learning spaces. Just as with thermal comfort and lighting controls, delivering high-performing interior acoustic environments adds to the satisfaction and well-being of building occupants and employees (Figure 10.14).

Strategies

The *Green Building and LEED Core Concepts Guide* provides the following strategies to address acoustics and therefore increase occupant comfort[11]:

1. *Consider acoustical impacts.* Consider interior finishes, building geometry, and duct insulation that will impact the ability for employees and staff to communicate and work effectively.

2. *Conduct occupant surveys.* Discover the overall satisfaction of the interior acoustic quality of the majority of the occupants to determine areas for improvement.

TIP Create a flashcard to remember the two strategies to improve acoustics in reference to IEQ.

QUIZ TIME!

Q10.11. A tenant fit-out project seeking LEED CI certification plans to use a raised access floor to include underfloor air distribution, allowing the use of floor-mounted operable diffusers at each workstation and therefore eliminating overhead ducts, thus maximizing the interior floor-to-ceiling height. The moderate supply air temperature required at the diffusers would reduce the amount of

Figure 10.14 Designing for proper acoustic performance also helps to improve the satisfaction and comfort levels of occupants by improving the ability to effectively communicate. *Photo courtesy of Steelcase, Inc.*

energy associated with cooling a consistently greater quantity of outside air needed to improve air quality. Which LEED strategies are addressed? (Choose two)

A. Increased Ventilation

B. Construction IAQ Management

C. Regional Priority

D. Controllability of Systems: Thermal Comfort

E. Acoustical Performance

Q10.12. Which of the following design-team deliverables and team members are most likely to play a significant role in achieving a Construction IAQ Management Plan? (Choose two)

A. Project specifications

B. Civil engineer

C. Construction documents

D. Lighting designer

E. General contractor

F. Electrical engineer

Q10.13. Which of the following most closely represents an appropriate level of overall illumination on an office work surface, including daylighting, ambient artificial lighting, and task lighting? (Choose one)

    A. 1–2 footcandles

    B. 5–10 footcandles

    C. 15–25 footcandles

    D. 40–60 footcandles

    E. 75–120 footcandles

    F. 150–200 footcandles

Q10.14. To which standards should engineers design the ventilation systems for a LEED project? (Choose two)

    A. ASHRAE 55

    B. California Air Resources Board

    C. ASHRAE 62.1

    D. ASHRAE 90.1

    E. ASTM 44

Q10.15. Which of the following strategies have proven to increase productivity and occupant satisfaction in green buildings? (Choose two)

    A. Providing access to daylight

    B. Selecting a site adjacent to a shopping center

    C. Improving indoor air quality

    D. Implementing a recycling program

    E. Offering incentives for carpooling

Q10.16. A mid-sized hotel project plans on incorporating appropriate passive-solar orientation, geometry, and glazing to minimize summer cooling loads and to take advantage of the site's opportunities for winter solar gain. The building will be built from 8-inch-thick structural insulated panels (SIPs) with a pressed straw insulated core held together by the natural resins from the straw and using face sheets of exterior-grade OSB made from 100 percent preconsumer scrap wood and a phenol-formaldehyde-based resin. Which of the following LEED credits would these strategies contribute? (Choose three)

    A. Local/Regional Materials

    B. Low-Emitting Materials: Adhesives & Sealants

C. Optimized Energy Performance

D. Low-Emitting Materials: Composite Wood

E. Low-Emitting Materials: Paints & Coatings

F. Recycled Content

G. Minimum Acoustical Performance

CHAPTER **11**

INNOVATION IN DESIGN AND REGIONAL PRIORITY

THE PREVIOUS FIVE CHAPTERS detailed the main categories of the Leadership in Energy and Environmental Design (LEED®) rating systems, while this chapter focuses on the two bonus categories of the rating systems: Innovation in Design (ID) and Regional Priority (RP). These categories are treated as bonus categories, as neither contains any prerequisites. The ID category encourages projects to explore new and innovative strategies and technologies, while the RP category offers additional point–earning opportunities focused on geographic environmental achievements.

Remember to switch back to the white flashcards for ID and RP topics.

INNOVATION IN DESIGN

The Innovation in Design category encourages the exploration and implementation of new green building technologies, as well as exceeding the thresholds defined in the existing LEED credits. The LEED rating systems offer up to five points for projects within the ID category by addressing three different strategies:

A. Exemplary Performance

B. Innovation in Design

C. Including a LEED Accredited Professional on the project team

Create a flashcard to remember the three strategies to earn ID points.

   Three of the five available ID points can be used toward the achievement of Exemplary Performance. Exemplary Performance credits are achieved once projects surpass the minimum performance-based thresholds defined in the existing LEED credits, typically the next incremental percentage threshold. For example, projects can earn exemplary performance credits (within the ID category) for achieving the following:

■ Diverting 95 percent of construction waste

■ Reducing water consumption by more than 40 percent

■ When 30 percent or more of material costs include products purchased within 500 miles

   If the team uses all three opportunities for exemplary performance achievements, they still have two more point opportunities for implementing innovative strategies. If the team pursues less than three credits within the ID category for exemplary performance, then they can pursue more innovative strategies. The

Remember the cradle-to-grave cycle from Chapter 9? C2C products are not only made of recycled products, but are recyclable after their useful life to avoid landfills and incineration facilities.

Remember what fly ash is from Chapter 9?

teams should research credit interpretation requests (CIRs) to see if their proposed strategy has been incorporated or presented in the past, or issue a new CIR to inquire about the award potential. Some examples previously submitted and awarded include:

- Incorporating cradle-to-cradle (C2C) certified products (Figure 11.1)
- Implementing an educational program for occupants and visitors (Figure 11.2)
- Using large amounts of fly ash in concrete
- Achieving LEED credits from other rating systems, such as Acoustical Performance from LEED for Schools

The LEED rating systems also offer another point opportunity for including a LEED Accredited Professional (AP) on the project team. Including a LEED AP on the project team can add efficiencies, as they are aware of the requirements of the LEED certification process. They are familiar with integrated design processes and understand how to evaluate the trade-offs and synergies of green building strategies and technologies. For the purposes of the exam, it is critical to remember only **one point** can be awarded to projects for this credit; it does not matter how many LEED APs are on the project team, just as long as there is one. Unfortunately, LEED Green Associates do not qualify for the extra point under this credit.

The LEED for Existing Buildings: Operations & Maintenance™ (EBOM) rating system actually offers only four points for Innovation (in Operations), including three for Exemplary Performance. To make up the point difference, the EBOM rating system offers another point opportunity for documenting sustainable building cost impacts.

Figure 11.1 C2C products help to extend the life of materials, although repurposed, reducing the need for virgin materials. *Photo courtesy of Steelcase, Inc.*

Figure 11.2 Providing opportunities to educate the end users and community about the benefits and strategies of green building helps to further transform the market and therefore contributes to earning LEED certification. *Photo courtesy of Rainwater HOG, LLC*

REGIONAL PRIORITY

The Regional Priority category offers the opportunity to earn bonus points for achieving compliance of previously mentioned existing LEED credits. U.S. Green Building Council's (USGBC's®) eight Regional Councils consulted with the local chapters to determine which existing LEED credits are more challenging to achieve within certain zip codes. Based on the results of their findings, USGBC compiled a database of all the zip codes in the United States (available on the USGBC website) and chose six existing LEED credits to coordinate with each corresponding geographic region. For example, a project located in Dania Beach, Florida, could earn a bonus point within the RP category for purchasing 20 percent of their materials within 500 miles from the project site, as USGBC has recognized in South Florida few opportunities exist to obtain building materials within 500 miles! A project could earn up to four Regional Priority credits (RPCs) out of the six opportunities presented. For the purposes of the exam, it is critical to remember that RPCs are not new credits.

 Do you remember the point structure for the different certification levels of LEED? How many points does a project need to achieve to earn Platinum status?

QUIZ TIME!

Q11.1. Exemplary performance generally requires which of the following? (Choose one)

A. Develop an innovative strategy not presented in any existing LEED credit.

B. Achieve either 20 percent or the next incremental percentage threshold established by the existing LEED credit that is being exceeded, whichever is greater.

    C. Meet or exceed the next percentage threshold as listed within the existing credit.

    D. Surpass the defined threshold of an innovative strategy being proposed by the team.

    E. Regardless of the LEED credit being pursued, achieve at least double the minimum effort described within the existing LEED credit, regardless of which credit is being exceeded.

Q11.2. Pursuing an Innovation in Design opportunity is appropriate when *at least one* of which of the following are true? (Choose two)

    A. The project is unable to meet the requirements established by an existing LEED credit.

    B. The compliance paths offered within an existing LEED credit are not possible to pursue.

    C. The project has exceeded or is projected to exceed the minimum performance established by an existing LEED credit.

    D. The project has achieved measurable performance in a LEED credit within another rating system.

Q11.3. Is it possible for the same building to earn multiple LEED certifications?

    A. Yes

    B. No

Q11.4. Which of the following statements are true regarding RPCs? (Choose three)

    A. Earning an RPC adds a bonus point to the project's total points.

    B. RPCs are new credits included in the LEED rating systems.

    C. Projects that are not registered with the 2009 versions of LEED are not awarded points within the Regional Priority category.

    D. Each zip code is assigned eight RPC opportunities.

    E. A project may earn up to four RPC bonus points.

Q11.5. How many points can be earned in the Regional Priority category?

    A. Six

    B. Three

    C. Two

    D. Four

    E. Ten

Q11.6. There are five LEED APs on the Botanical Center project, including three from the architectural firm, one from the mechanical engineering firm, and another one from the electrical engineering firm. How many points can be achieved within the ID category for achieving this effort?

A. One

B. Two

C. Three

D. Four

PART III

STUDY
TIPS AND
APPENDICES

CHAPTER **12**

STUDY TIPS

AS MENTIONED EARLIER IN THE INTRODUCTION OF THIS BOOK, this chapter is dedicated to providing an approach for the rest of your study efforts during Week Five. It includes tips for taking online practice exams and resources on where to find additional information while you continue to study, as well as providing an insight to the Prometric testing center environment and the exam format structure.

PREPARING FOR THE LEED® GREEN ASSOCIATE EXAM: WEEK FIVE

By the time you read this section, it should be Week Five of your study efforts. You should have your white set of flashcards covering the basics of Leadership in Energy and Environmental Design (LEED®) (including Innovation in Design [ID] and Regional Priority [RP] bonus categories) and your color-coded cards separated into the five main categories of the LEED rating systems. This week will be a great opportunity to rewrite your cheat sheet at least three times. Note, your cheat sheet may evolve as you take a few online practice exams.

During Week Five, you may need to reference additional resources while studying. For example, if you want to learn more about the cost implications of LEED projects, refer to *Cost of Green Revisited* by Davis Langdon. Although a sample credit is provided in Appendix G of this book on page 162, I would recommend downloading the primary reference, the *LEED for Homes™ Rating System*, and skim through it to see how the categories, prerequisites, and credits are organized and presented. I would also recommend reading through two more primary references: the *CIR Guidelines* and *Guidance on ID Credits*. All of these references are available to download from the *LEED Green Associate Candidate Handbook* on the GBCI website for free. Again, it is highly recommended to download the most current *Candidate Handbook* from the GBCI website, but as a point of reference, at the time of printing the primary references included:

- *Green Building and LEED Core Concepts Guide*, 1st ed. (USGBC, 2009)
- *Green Office Guide: Integrating LEED Into Your Leasing Process*, Section 2.4 (USGBC, 2009)
- *LEED 2009 for New Construction and Major Renovations Rating System* (USGBC, 2009)
- *LEED for Existing Buildings: Operations & Maintenance Reference Guide*, Introduction (USGBC, 2008)
- *LEED for Existing Buildings: Operations & Maintenance Reference Guide*, Glossary (USGBC, 2008)
- *LEED for Homes Rating System* (USGBC, 2008)

 TIP Download and read through three of the primary references from the *Green Associate Candidate Handbook*:

- LEED for Homes Rating System, Introduction
- CIR Guidelines
- Guidance on ID Credits

- *Cost of Green Revisited*, by Davis Langdon (2007)
- *Sustainable Building Technical Manual: Part II*, by Anthony Bernheim and William Reed (1996)
- *The Treatment by LEED® of the Environmental Impact of HVAC Refrigerants* (LEED Technical and Scientific Advisory Committee, 2004)
- *Guidance on Innovation & Design (ID) Credits* (USGBC, 2004)
- *Guidelines for CIR Customers* (USGBC, 2007)

The ancillary references at the time of printing included:

- *Energy Performance of LEED® for New Construction Buildings: Final Report*, by Cathy Turner and Mark Frankel (2008)
- *Foundations of the Leadership in Energy and Environmental Design Environmental Rating System: A Tool for Market Transformation* (LEED Steering Committee, 2006)
- *AIA Integrated Project Delivery: A Guide* (www.aia.org)
- *Review of ANSI/ASHRAE Standard 62.1-2004: Ventilation for Acceptable Indoor Air Quality*, by Brian Kareis (www.workplacegroup.net)
- *Best Practices of ISO 14021: Self-Declared Environmental Claims*, by Kun-Mo Lee and Haruo Uehara (2003)
- Bureau of Labor Statistics (www.bls.gov)
- International Code Council (www.iccsafe.org)
- Americans with Disabilities Act (ADA): Standards for Accessible Design (www.ada.gov)
- *GSA 2003 Facilities Standards* (General Services Administration, 2003)
- *Guide to Purchasing Green Power* (Environmental Protection Agency, 2004)
- *LEED 2009 for Operations & Maintenance Rating System* (USGBC, 2009)

Some other resources include:

- www.usgbc.org. You may want to check out some of the rating system scorecards or read about credit weightings of LEED v3. The USGBC® website is also your primary source to learn about any updates to the LEED rating systems.
- www.gbci.org. Make sure you download the current *Candidate Handbook*, and you may want to reference the Disciplinary Policy, the Minimum Program Requirements, and the project registration information.
- www.leedonline.com. Even if you do not have any projects assigned to you, you will still be able to see what it looks like and watch a demo video.

Practice Exam Approach

Also during Week Five, you should take some online practice exams. Although there are many sample exam questions provided in this book, it is helpful to practice for the real-life testing environment scenario. Search online, as you will find that there are a few options from which to choose. When you are taking a practice exam, pretend as if it is the real thing. For example, time yourself, have scratch paper and a pencil available, make a cheat sheet in about two to three minutes, do not use this book or your flashcards, and avoid any disruptions. Most of the online practice exams allow you to flag questions you are doubtful of, so take advantage of this for practice.

Most of the questions include multiple choices with multiple answers required. When approaching these types of questions, it is best advised to hide or cover up the provided answer options and formulate your own answers to help avoid getting sidetracked by the answer selection choices. Once you uncover or reveal the answer choices, make sure to read through all of the options before selecting your final answer(s). Be sure to read each question carefully and select the proper number of answers. After taking the practice exam, go through the answer key and evaluate your score. On the first practice exam, read through each question and answer one by one to understand how you decided on the correct answer and where you went wrong on the incorrect ones. Try to notice a pattern on your strengths and weaknesses to determine where your study efforts need to be devoted to improve your score. After taking the first practice exam, you may just want to focus on the questions you answered incorrectly.

THE TESTING CENTER ENVIRONMENT

The introduction of this book described the opportunity to make a cheat sheet after you completed the tutorial at the testing center, and Chapter 1 detailed how to schedule your exam date with a Prometric testing center. Hopefully, your exam date is still not scheduled at this point, as one more week of prep time is suggested to review your flashcards, refine your cheat sheet, and have the opportunity to take a few online practice exams. As stated earlier, it is best to assess your knowledge before scheduling your exam date.

TIP Be sure to visit www.GreenEDU .com to take online practice exams to simulate your exam day environment.

During Week Six, the week of your test date, there are a few things to remember before you sit for the exam:

- Remember to visit the GBCI website and download the latest version of the *LEED Green Associate Candidate Handbook.*

- Confirm your exam date at least one day prior.

- Find the Prometric testing center and map your path to make sure you know where you are going on your exam day.

- Keep rewriting your cheat sheet and studying your flashcards. Take your flashcards everywhere with you!

To be prepared on the day of your exam, please note the following:

- Bring your picture ID with matching name, just as it is on your GBCI profile.

- Dress comfortably and bring a sweater or a jacket, as the testing center may be cold.

- Be sure to get plenty of rest and eat something, as you will not want to take any breaks during the exam to grab a bite or a drink (the clock cannot be paused).

- Be sure to check in at least 30 minutes prior to your testing time. If you miss your scheduled exam time, you will be considered absent and will have to forfeit your exam fees and the opportunity to take the exam.

- Be sure to use the restroom after checking in and prior to being escorted to your workstation. Remember, no breaks!

■ You will be observed during your testing session and will be audio and video recorded as well.

■ You will not be allowed to bring any personal items to your workstation such as calculators, paper, pencils, purses, wallets, food, or books.

EXAM STRUCTURE

 TIP The formulas and an on-screen calculator will be provided should you be required to perform any calculations.

The exam is structured to test you on three components, as described in the *Candidate Handbook* provided by GBCI. You will be tested on recognition items, application items, and analysis items. The recognition items test your ability to remember factual data once presented in a similar environment to the exam references. For example, you may need to provide the definition for a term or recall a fact. The application items present a situation for you to solve using the principles and elements described in the exam format. These questions may require you to perform a calculation or provide the process or sequence of actions (i.e., CIRs, registration, certification). The analysis items are presented to evaluate your ability to evaluate a problem to create a solution. These question types are more challenging, as you must be able to decipher the different components of the problem and also assess the relationships of the components.

TIP Remember, the exam is composed of multiple-choice questions. No written answers are required!

The exam questions are separated into categories of focus areas and then are coordinated with an applicable rating system category. For example, project site factors coordinate with the Sustainable Sites (SS) category, and water management issues coordinate with the Water Efficiency (WE) category. Project systems and energy impacts coordinate with the Energy & Atmosphere (EA) category while acquisition, installation, and management of project materials coordinate with the Materials & Resources (MR) category. Improvements to the indoor environment coordinate with the Indoor Environmental Quality (IEQ) category. Stakeholder involvement in innovation, project surroundings, and public outreach coordinate with the Innovation in Design (ID) and Regional Priority (RP) categories. Therefore, you should be familiar with each of the credit categories as presented earlier in Part II, Chapters 6 through 11.

When at the Testing Center

To give you an idea of what to expect, once you are at your workstation:

■ You should dedicate 2 hours and 20 minutes to take the exam:

  ■ 10-minute tutorial

  ■ 2-hour exam

  ■ 10-minute exit survey

■ The tutorial is computer based so make sure your workstation's monitor, keyboard, and mouse are all functioning properly. After completing the tutorial, remember to then create your cheat sheet in the time left over.

■ The 2-hour exam is composed of 100 multiple-choice questions. Just like with the practice exam questions, in order for the question to be counted as CORRECT, you must select **all** of the correct answers within each question, as there is no partial credit for choosing two out of the three correct answers.

- Although some of the practice exam questions in this book are formatted with a true or false statement or "All of the above" as an answer selection, you are less likely to find this on the real exam, as the questions tend to be straightforward and clear, to avoid any confusion.

- You will not see any credit numbers listed on their own, as all credit names will include the full name.

- Appendix J includes a list of commonly used acronyms. Although most of them are spelled out on the exam, it is still helpful to know what they are!

- During the exam, you will have the opportunity to mark or flag questions to come back to later. It is advised that you take advantage of this, as you may be short on time and want to revisit only the questions you were doubtful about. Please note, any unanswered questions are marked INCORRECT, so it is best to at least try.

TIP Remember to rely on your instincts. Typically, the first answer that comes to mind is often the right one!

- The 10-minute exit survey is followed by your exam results … yes, instant and immediate results!

Exam Scoring

The exams are scored on a scale from 125 to 200, where 170+ is considered passing. Please do not worry about how the questions are weighted, just do your best! Should you need to retake the exam, your application is valid for one year and therefore you will have three chances within the year to earn a score of 170 or more. Please consult the *Candidate Handbook* for more information.

After the Exam

Once you have passed the LEED Green Associate exam, remember to change your signature to reflect earning the credential! Remember, it is not appropriate to use "LEED GA," but instead use "LEED Green Associate." Although your certificate will not arrive immediately, remember—you must fulfill 15 hours of continuing education over the next two years. Please refer to the Credential Maintenance Program (CMP) handbook found on the GBCI website for more information. There is also a code of conduct you must abide by, as stipulated in the Disciplinary Policy posted on the GBCI website at www.gbci.org/Files/Disc_ExamAppeals_Policy.pdf. It states individuals with LEED credentials must:

A. Be truthful, forthcoming, and cooperative in their dealings with GBCI.

B. Be in continuous compliance with GBCI rules (as amended from time to time by GBCI).

 TIP The Disciplinary Policy found on the GBCI website also includes the Exam Appeals Policy if needed.

C. Respect GBCI intellectual property rights.

D. Abide by laws related to the profession and to general public health and safety.

E. Carry out their professional work in a competent and objective manner.

Appendix A

RATING SYSTEMS OVERVIEW

Overview of the LEED® Rating Systems

REFERENCE GUIDE	RATING SYSTEM	APPLICABLE PROJECT TYPES
BD+C	**New Construction (NC)**	
		• New buildings
		• Major renovations: HVAC, envelope and interior habilitation
		• Commercial occupancies: offices, institutional, hotels, residential with four or more stories
		• Shared tenant space: occupy more than 50 percent of leasable SF
	Core & Shell (CS)	
		• Developer controls core and shell but not tenant fit-out
		• Commercial and medical office buildings, retail centers, warehouses
		• Shared tenant space: occupy less than 50 percent of leasable SF
	Schools	
		• K–12 typically
		• New schools and renovations of existing
		• Following can be used for either LEED for Schools or NC:
		– Nonacademic buildings: admin offices, maintenance facilities, dorms
		– Postsecondary academic and prekindergarten buildings
	Health Care	
	New Construction: Retail	

GBOM	**Existing Buildings: Operations & Maintenance (EBOM)**	
		• Applies to buildings new to LEED or previously certified under NC, CS, or Schools
		• Commercial occupancies: offices, institutional, hotels, residential with four or more stories
		• Applicable for:
		– Building operations
		– Process and system upgrades
		– Minor space-use changes, facility alterations, and additions
		• Individual tenant spaces do not apply

REFERENCE GUIDE	RATING SYSTEM	APPLICABLE PROJECT TYPES
ID+C	**Existing Schools**	
	Commercial Interiors (CI)	
		• For tenant spaces:
		– Office, retail, and institutional
		– Tenant spaces that don't occupy entire building
		• Works hand-in-hand with LEED CS
	Retail Interiors	

HOMES	**Homes**	
		• New residences and major remodels
		– Single-family, low-rise multifamily, affordable housing, production, manufactured and modular housing

ND	**Neighborhood Development (ND)**	
		• For developmental projects:
		– Neighborhoods (whole, fraction, or multiple)
		– Smaller infill projects
		– Larger mixed-use developments

Appendix B

MINIMUM PROGRAM REQUIREMENTS (MPRs)

Minimum Program Requirements (MPRs)

1	MUST COMPLY WITH ENVIRONMENTAL LAWS
NC, CS, SCHOOLS, CI	Must comply with all applicable federal, state, and local building-related environmental laws and regulations in place where the project is located.
	This condition must be satisfied from the date of or the initiation of schematic design, whichever comes first, until the date that the building receives a certificate of occupancy or similar official indication that it is ready for use.
EBOM	Must comply with all applicable federal, state, and local building-related environmental laws and regulations in place where the project is located.
	This condition must be satisfied from the start of the LEED project's first LEED EB: O&M performance period through the expiration date of the LEED certification.
2	**MUST BE A COMPLETE, PERMANENT BUILDING OR SPACE**
ALL	All LEED projects must be designed for, constructed on, and operated on a permanent location on already existing land.
	No building or space that is designed to move at any point in its lifetime may pursue LEED certification.
NC, CS, SCHOOLS	LEED projects must include the new, ground-up design and construction, or major renovation, of at least one building in its entirety.
	Construction prerequisites and credits may not be submitted for review until substantial completion of construction has occurred.
CI	The LEED project scope must include a complete interior space distinct from other spaces within the same building with regard to at least one of the following characteristics: ownership, management, lease, or party wall separation.
	Construction prerequisites and credits may not be submitted for review until substantial completion of construction has occurred.
EBOM	LEED projects must include at least one existing building in its entirety.
3	**MUST USE A REASONABLE SITE BOUNDARY**
NC, CS, SCHOOLS, EBOM	1. The LEED project boundary must include all contiguous land that is associated with and supports normal building operations for the LEED project building, including all land that was or will be disturbed for the purpose of undertaking the LEED project.
	2. The LEED project boundary may not include land that is owned by a party other than that which owns the LEED project unless that land is associated with and supports normal building operations for the LEED project building.
	3. LEED projects located on a campus must have project boundaries such that if all the buildings on campus become LEED certified, then 100 percent of the gross land area on the campus would be included within a LEED boundary. If this requirement is in conflict with MPR 7, Must Comply with Minimum Building Area to Site Area Ratio, then MPR 7 will take precedence.
	4. Any given parcel of real property may be attributed to only a single LEED project building.
	5. Gerrymandering of a LEED project boundary is prohibited: the boundary may not unreasonably exclude sections of land to create boundaries in unreasonable shapes for the sole purpose of complying with prerequisites or credits.

CI	If any land was or will be disturbed for the purpose of undertaking the LEED project, then that land must be included within the LEED project boundary.
4	**MUST COMPLY WITH MINIMUM FLOOR AREA REQUIREMENTS**
NC, CS, SCHOOLS, EBOM	The LEED project must include a minimum of 1,000 square feet of gross floor area.
CI	The LEED project must include a minimum of 250 square feet of gross floor area.
5	**MUST COMPLY WITH MINIMUM OCCUPANCY RATES**
NC, CS, SCHOOLS, CI	Full-time equivalent occupancy
	The LEED project must serve one or more full-time equivalent (FTE) occupant(s), calculated as an annual average in order to use LEED in its entirety. If the project serves less than one annualized FTE, optional credits from the Indoor Environmental Quality category may not be earned (the prerequisites must still be earned).
EBOM	Full-time equivalent occupancy
	The LEED project must serve one or more full-time equivalent (FTE) occupant(s), calculated as an annual average in order to use LEED in its entirety. If the project serves less than one annualized FTE, optional credits from the Indoor Environmental Quality category may not be earned (the prerequisites must still be earned).
	Minimum occupancy rate
	The LEED project must be in a state of typical physical occupancy, and all building systems must be operating at a capacity necessary to serve the current occupants, for a period that includes all performance periods as well as at least the 12 continuous months immediately preceding the first submission for a review.
6	**COMMITMENT TO SHARE WHOLE-BUILDING ENERGY AND WATER USAGE DATA**
ALL	All certified projects must commit to sharing with USGBC and/or GBCI all available actual whole-project energy and water usage data for a period of at least five years. This period starts on the date that the LEED project begins typical physical occupancy if certifying under NC, CS, Schools, or CI, or the date that the building is awarded certification if certifying under EBOM.
	This commitment must carry forward if the building or space changes ownership or lessee.
7	**MUST COMPLY WITH A MINIMUM BUILDING AREA TO SITE AREA RATIO**
ALL	The gross floor area of the LEED project building must be no less than 2 percent of the gross land area within the LEED project boundary.

Appendix C

LEED® CERTIFICATION PROCESS

The Basic Steps in the LEED Certification Process

PROJECT REGISTRATION	
	Access to LEED Online
	– LEED Scorecard
	– LEED Credit Submittal Templates
DESIGN APPLICATION PHASE (OPTIONAL)	
	Submit Credits and Prerequisites via LEED Online
	– Comes back "Anticipated" or "Denied" (25 days)
	– No points awarded
	Clarification Request (25 days)
	Final Design Review (15 days)
	– Project team can:
	– ACCEPT: goes to Construction Application phase
	– APPEAL: goes to Design Appeal phase
DESIGN APPEAL PHASE	
	Changes made and submitted once again
	– Comes back "Anticipated" or "Denied" (25 days)
	No clarification requests
	Final Design Review (15 days)
CONSTRUCTION APPLICATION PHASE	
	Submit via LEED Online (both design and construction)
	– Comes back "Anticipated" or "Denied" (25 days)
	– No points awarded yet
	Clarification Request (25 days)
	Final Construction Review (15 days)
	– Project team can:
	– ACCEPT: goes to Certification/Denial phase
	– APPEAL: goes to Construction Appeal phase

CONSTRUCTION APPEAL PHASE	
	Changes made and submitted once again
	– Comes back "Anticipated" or "Denied"
	No clarification requests
	Final Construction Review (15 days)
CERTIFIED/DENIAL PHASE	
	After Final Construction Review is ACCEPTED:
	– Certification Level Awards: Certified, Silver, Gold, or Platinum
	– Denied: project closed (appeals should be done in prior phases)

Appendix D

MAIN CATEGORY SUMMARIES

Sustainable Sites
  Site Selection
    Increase density
    Redevelopment
    Protect habitat
  Transportation
    Public Transportation
    Limit Parking Capacity
    Encourage Carpooling
    Low-Emitting and Fuel-Efficient Vehicles
    Alternative Incentive Strategies
Site Design & Management
    Minimize Building Footprint
    Minimize Hardscape
    Minimize Water Usage
    Use Reflective Materials
    Develop a Sustainable Management Plan
    Reduce Light Pollution
Stormwater Management
    Minimize Impervious Areas
    Control Stormwater
    Harvest Rainwater
Water Efficiency
  Indoor Water Use Reduction
    Efficient Plumbing Fixtures
    Use Nonpotable Water
    Submeters
  Outdoor Water Use Reduction
    Native and Adaptive Plants
    Xeriscaping
    Efficient Irrigation Systems
    Use Nonpotable Water
    Submeters
  Process Water
    Efficient Equipment & Appliances
    Use Nonpotable Water
    Submeters
Energy & Atmosphere
  Energy Demand
    Establish Design and Energy Goals

Size the Building Appropriately
Use Free Energy
Insulate
Monitor Consumption
  Energy Efficiency
    Identify Passive Design Opportunities
    Address the Envelope
    Install High-Performance Mechanical Systems
    Use High-Efficiency Appliances
    Use High-Efficiency Infrastructures
    Capture Efficiencies of Scale
    Use Thermal Energy Storage
    Use Energy Simulation
    Monitor and Verify Performance
  Renewable Energy
    On Site versus Off Site
  Ongoing Energy Performance
    Adhere to OPR
    Training for Staff
    Preventative Maintenance
    Incentives for Tenants and Occupants
Materials & Resources
  Building Material Life-Cycle Impacts
    Specify green materials
    Specify green interiors
    Specify green electronic equipment
  Waste Management
    Size the building appropriately
    Develop a construction waste management policy
    Encourage recycling
    Reuse or salvage building materials
    Reuse existing buildings
    Compost
    Consider new technology, design, and
      construction decisions
Indoor Environmental Quality
  Indoor Air Quality
    Prohibit Smoking
    Ensure adequate ventilation
    Monitor carbon dioxide

Install high-efficiency air filters
Specify low-emitting materials
Use integrated pest management
Protect air quality during construction
Conduct a flush-out
Employ a green cleaning program

Thermal Comfort

Install operable windows
Give occupants temperature and ventilation control
Conduct occupant surveys

Lighting

Use daylighting
Give occupants lighting control
Conduct occupant surveys

Acoustics

Consider acoustical impacts
Conduct occupant surveys

Appendix E

TRADE-OFFS AND SYNERGIES

Trade-Offs and Synergies Summary

STORMWATER MANAGEMENT
Synergies:
Reuse for flushing toilets or urinals
Reuse to water landscaping
Increase pervious pavement to recharge groundwater
Reduces pollutants from entering water bodies
CAPTURING RAINWATER
Synergies:
Reuse for flushing toilets or urinals
Reuse to water landscaping
Reduces stormwater runoff
CHOOSING A BROWNFIELD SITE OR PREVIOUSLY DEVELOPED SITE
Synergies:
Development density (infrastructure exists)
Community connectivity
Public transportation access
LIMIT PARKING
Synergies:
Helps to maximize open space
Reduces heat island effect
Stormwater management opportunities with paving materials
VEGETATED ROOF
Synergies:
Reduces stormwater runoff from roof
Reduces heat island effect
Provides thermal barrier to save energy
Qualifies as open space and preserved habitat
Trade-offs:
Can be costly and challenging to coordinate
Reduces the amount of rainwater to be captured for nonpotable water uses

WATER-EFFICIENT LANDSCAPING

Synergies:

Xeriscaping can provide buffers to help optimize energy performance

Xeriscaping can add efficiencies to passive designs

Vegetation can restore habitat

INCREASED VENTILATION

Synergies:

Improves air quality

Operable windows contribute to earning Thermal Comfort credit

Natural ventilation reduces operating costs

Trade-offs:

Requires mechanical systems to work harder to heat and cool

Increases HVAC capacity

Increases capital and operating costs

BUILDING AND MATERIAL REUSE

Synergies:

Reduces the need for virgin raw materials

Reduces burden on budget as new typically costs more

Can contribute to earning other points, such as Regional Materials

DAYLIGHTING

Synergies:

Reduces need for artificial lighting

Provides connection to exterior environment for occupants

Trade-offs:

Windows provide poor thermal break

Increases glare problems for occupants

Requires increased heating loads in winter and higher cooling loads in summer

PROVIDING OPERABLE WINDOWS

Synergies:

Increases natural ventilation

Operable windows contribute to earning the Thermal Comfort credit

Trade-offs:

Can cause acoustic issues

Appendix F

Project Name

Date

LEED 2009 for New Construction and Major Renovation
Project Checklist[1]

Sustainable Sites — 26 Possible Points

Yes ? No

Prereq 1	Construction Activity Pollution Prevention	Required
Credit 1	Site Selection	1
Credit 2	Development Density & Community Connectivity	5
Credit 3	Brownfield Redevelopment	1
Credit 4.1	Alternative Transportation, Public Transportation Access	6
Credit 4.2	Alternative Transportation, Bicycle Storage & Changing Rooms	1
Credit 4.3	Alternative Transportation, Low-Emitting & Fuel-Efficient Vehicles	3
Credit 4.4	Alternative Transportation, Parking Capacity	2
Credit 5.1	Site Development, Protection of Restore Habitat	1
Credit 5.2	Site Development, Maximize Open Space	1
Credit 6.1	Stormwater Design, Quantity Control	1
Credit 6.2	Stormwater Design, Quality Control	1
Credit 7.1	Heat Island Effect, Non-Roof	1
Credit 7.2	Heat Island Effect, Roof	1
Credit 8	Light Pollution Reduction	1

Water Efficiency — 10 Possible Points

Prereq 1	Water Use Reduction – 20% Reduction	Required
Credit 1	Water Efficient Landscaping	2 to 4
Credit 2	Innovative Wastewater Technologies	2
Credit 3	Water Use Reduction	2 to 4

Energy & Atmosphere — 35 Possible Points

Prereq 1	Fundamental Commissioning of Building Energy Systems	Required
Prereq 2	Minimum Energy Performance	Required
Prereq 3	Fundamental Refrigerant Management	Required
Credit 1	Optimize Energy Performance	1 to 19
Credit 2	On-Site Renewable Energy	1 to 7
Credit 3	Enhanced Commissioning	2
Credit 4	Enhanced Refrigerant Management	2
Credit 5	Measurement & Verification	3
Credit 6	Green Power	2

Materials & Resources — 14 Possible Points

Prereq 1	Storage & Collection of Recyclables	Required
Credit 1.1	Building Reuse, Maintain Existing Walls, Floors & Roof	1 to 3
Credit 1.2	Building Reuse, Maintain 50% of Interior Non-Structural Elements	1
Credit 2	Construction Waste Management	1 to 2
Credit 3	Materials Reuse	1 to 2

Materials & Resources, Continued — 14 Possible Points

Credit 4	Recyled Content	1 to 2
Credit 5	Regional Materials	1 to 2
Credit 6	Rapidly Renewable Materials	1
Credit 7	Certified Wood	1

Indoor Environmental Quality — 15 Possible Points

Prereq 1	Minimum Indoor Air Quality Performance	Required
Prereq 2	Environmental Tobacco Smoke (ETS) Control	Required
Credit 1	Outdoor Air Delivery Monitoring	1
Credit 2	Increased Ventilation	1
Credit 3.1	Construction IAQ Management Plan – During Construction	1
Credit 3.2	Construction IAQ Management Plan – Before Occupancy	1
Credit 4.1	Low-Emitting Materials, Adhesives & Sealants	1
Credit 4.2	Low-Emitting Materials, Paints & Coatings	1
Credit 4.3	Low-Emitting Materials, Flooring Systems	1
Credit 4.4	Low-Emitting Materials, Composite Wood & Agrifiber Products	1
Credit 5	Indoor Chemical & Pollutant Source Control	1
Credit 6.1	Controllability of Systems, Lighting	1
Credit 6.2	Controllability of Systems, Thermal Comfort	1
Credit 7.1	Thermal Comfort, Design	1
Credit 7.2	Thermal Comfort, Verification	1
Credit 8.1	Daylight & Views, Daylight	1
Credit 8.2	Daylight & Views, Views	1

Innovation and Design Process — 6 Possible Points

Credit 1.1	Innovation or Exemplary Performance	1
Credit 1.2	Innovation or Exemplary Performance	1
Credit 1.3	Innovation or Exemplary Performance	1
Credit 1.4	Innovation	1
Credit 1.5	Innovation	1
Credit 2	LEED® Accredited Professional	1

Regional Priority Credits — 4 Possible Points

Credit 1.1	Regional Priority: Specific Credit	1
Credit 1.2	Regional Priority: Specific Credit	1
Credit 1.3	Regional Priority: Specific Credit	1
Credit 1.4	Regional Priority: Specific Credit	1

Total — 110 Possible Points

Certified: 40 to 49 points, **Silver:** 50 to 59 points, **Gold:** 60 to 79 points, **Platinum:** 80 to 110 points

Appendix G

SAMPLE CREDIT

MR CREDIT 5: REGIONAL MATERIALS

1–2 Points

Intent

To increase demand for building materials and products that are extracted and manufactured within the region, thereby supporting the use of indigenous resources and reducing the environmental impacts resulting from transportation.

Requirements

Use building materials or products that have been extracted, harvested or recovered, as well as manufactured within 500 miles of the project site for a minimum of 10 percent or 20 percent, based on cost, of the total materials value. If only a fraction of a product or material is extracted, harvested, or recovered and manufactured locally, then only that percentage (by weight) can contribute to the regional value. The minimum percentage regional materials for each point threshold is as follows:

Regional Materials	Points
10%	1
20%	2

Mechanical, electrical, and plumbing components and specialty items such as elevators and equipment must not be included in this calculation. Include only materials permanently installed in the project. Furniture may be included if it is included consistently in MR Credit 3: Materials Reuse through MR Credit 7: Certified Wood.

Potential Technologies and Strategies

Establish a project goal for locally sourced materials, and identify materials and materials suppliers that can achieve this goal. During construction, ensure that the specified local materials are installed, and quantify the total percentage of local materials installed. Consider a range of environmental, economic, and performance attributes when selecting products and materials.

Appendix H

TRADITIONAL PROJECT DELIVERY VERSUS INTEGRATIVE PROJECT DELIVERY

Traditional/Conventional Projects versus Integrative Design

	CONVENTIONAL PROJECTS	**INTEGRATIVE DESIGN**
Teams:	Fragmented	Collaborative and collective
Process:	Linear and segregated	Integrated and holistic
Risk:	Individually managed	Collectively managed
Compensation:	Minimum effort for biggest return	
	FIRST-COST BASED	**VALUE-BASED**
Communication:	Analog	Digital
Technology:	Paper-based, 2D	3D, BIM
Contracts/Agreements:	Unilateral	Multilateral
Project Phases:	Predesign/Programming	Conceptualization
	Schematic Design	Criteria Design
	Design Development	Detailed Design
	Construction Documents	Implementation Documents
	Agency Permit/Bidding	Agency Coordination/Permit
	Construction	Construction
	Substantial Completion	Substantial Completion
	Final Completion	Final Completion
	Certificate of Occupancy	Certificate of Occupancy

Appendix I

REFERENCED STANDARDS

Referenced Standards for the LEED® Green Associate Exam

KEYWORDS	STANDARD
Stormwater Management Guide	EPA, Construction General Permit
Site Selection	USDA Definition of Prime Agricultural Land (US CFR)
	FEMA 100-Year Flood Definition
	Endangered Species Lists (U.S. Fish & Wildlife Service)
	National Marine Fisheries Services, List of Endangered Marine Species
	U.S. Code of Federal Regulations, Definition of Wetland (CFR)
	Definitions of Wetlands in the US CFR (40 CFR, Parts 230–233, 22)
Brownfield Redevelopment	ASTM E1527-05 Phase I Environmental Site Assessment
Site Assessment	ASTM E1903-97 Phase II Environmental Site Analysis
	EPA Brownfields Definition
Alternative Transportation	Institute of Transportation Engineers, Parking Generation Study, 2003
ZEV	California Air Resources Board (CARB)—Definition of ZEV (zero emission vehicle)
Green score	American Council for Energy Efficient Economy (ACEEE)
	SCAQMD, Rule 2202, On-Road Motor Vehicle Mitigation Options Employee Commute Reducation Program Guidelines, Chapter II, Feb 2004
Stormwater Mgmt: Quality Control	Guidance Specifying Mgmt Measures for Sources of Non-Point Pollution in Coastal Waters (US EPA 840B92002)
	National Technical Information Service (PB93234672)
Heat Island Effect	ASTM E408-71—Total Normal Emittance of Surfaces Using Inspection Meter
	ASTM C1371-04a—Determination of Emittance of Materials Near Room Temp
	ASTM E903-96—Solar Absorbance, Reflectance, and Transmittance Integrating Sphere
	ASTM E1918-97—Solar Reflectance of Horizontal and Low-Sloped Surfaces in Field
	ASTM C1549-04—Determination of Solar Reflectance Near Ambient Temperature
Light Pollution Reduction	ASHRAE/IESNA 90.1-2007 (Lighting, Section 9 without amendments)

WE

KEYWORDS	STANDARD
Water Use Reduction	Energy Policy Act (EPAct) 1992 became law in 2005
	Energy Policy Act (EPAct) 2005
	International Association of Plumbing & Mechanical Officials Publication (IAPMO)
	ICC, International Plumbing Code (IPC), 2006

EA

KEYWORDS	STANDARD
Minimum Energy Performance, Envelope, Bldg. Energy Systems	ASHRAE/IESNA 90.1-2007
Optimize Energy Performance, HVAC, Bldg. Energy Systems, Unitary Heating	ASHRAE Advanced Energy Design Guide for Small Office Buildings, 2006
	ASHRAE Advanced Energy Design Guide for Retail Buildings, 2006
	ASHRAE Advanced Energy Design Guide for Small Warehouses and Self-Storage Buildings, 2008
	ASHRAE Advanced Energy Design Guide for K–12 School Buildings
	NBI, Advanced Buildings™ Core Performance™ Guide
	ENERGY STAR Program, Target Finder Rating Tool
Optimize Energy Performance	ENERGY STAR Portfolio Manager
O+M, BMPs, Energy Performance	ASHRAE Level I, Walk-Through Analysis
O+M, BMPs, Energy Performance, Commissioning	ASHRAE Level II, Energy Audit: Energy Survey and Analysis
Refrigerant Mgmt, CFCs, HCFCs, HFCs	US EPA Clean Air Act, Title VI, Section 608, Refrigerant Recycling Rule
On-Site Renewable Energy	ASHRAE/IESNA 90.1-2007
Measurement & Verification	IPMVP, Jan 2006
Green Power, RECs	Center for Resource Solutions Green-e Product Certification Requirements

MR

KEYWORDS	STANDARD
Recycled Content	International Standard ISO 14021-1999—Environmental Labels and Declarations
Sustainable & Durable Goods	Electronic Product Environmental Assessment Tool (EPEAT)
Certified Wood, COCs, Forest Management	Forest Stewardship Council's Principles and Criteria
ENERGY STAR Equipment & Products	ENERGY STAR—Qualified Products
Reduced Mercury in Lamps	NEMA Voluntary Commitment on Mercury in Compact Fluorescent Lights
Food	Fairtrade Labeling Organizations (FLO) International Certifications
	Food Alliance Certification
	Marine Stewardship Council (MSC) Blue Eco-Label
	Protected Harvest Certification
	Rainforest Alliance Certification
	USDA Organic Certification

IEQ

KEYWORDS	STANDARD
IAQ	Indoor Air Quality Building Education and Assessment Model (I-BEAM)
IAQ, Natural Ventilation	ASHRAE 62.1-2007—Ventilation for Acceptable Indoor Air Quality
Environmental Tobacco Smoke Control, IAQ	ANSI/ASTM E779-03, Standard Test Method for Determining Air Leakage Rate by Fan Pressurization
	California Residential Alternative Calculation Method Approval Manual, HERS Required Verification and Diagnostic Testing
	Residential Manual for Compliance w/ CA's 2001 Energy Efficiency Standards, Chapter 4
	California Energy Commission
Acoustical Performance, Schools	ANSI/ASHRAE S12.60-2002, Design Requirements and Guidelines for Schools
	ASHRAE Handbook, Chapter 47, Sound and Vibration Control, 2003, HVAC
Increased Ventilation	The Carbon Trust Good Practice Guide 237—Natural Ventilation in Non-Domestic Buildings—a Guide for Designers, Developers, and Owners, 1998
	CIBSE Applications Manual 10: 2005, Natural Ventilation in Non-Domestic Buildings
Construction IAQ Management, Pollutant Control, MERV	ANSI/ASHRAE 52.2-1999—Method of Testing General Ventilation Air-Cleaning Devices for Removal Efficiency by Particle Size IAQ Guidelines for Occupied Buildings Under Construction, SMACNA
	US EPA Compendium of Methods for the Determination of Air Pollutants in Indoor Air

IEQ

KEYWORDS	STANDARD
VOCs, IAQ, Low-Emitting Materials	California Dept of Health Services
Low-Emitting Materials, Adhesives and Sealants, IAQ	South Coast Rule 1168, South Coast Air Quality Management District (SCAQMD), Jan 2005
	Green Seal Standard 36 (GS-36) Commercial Adhesives
Low-Emitting Materials, Paints and Coatings, IAQ	South Coast Air Quality Management District (SCAQMD) Rule 1113, Coatings
	Green Seal Standard 03 (GC-03) anti-corrosive and anti-rust paints
	Green Seal Standard 11 (GS-11) commercial flat and non-flat paints
Low-Emitting Materials, Carpet, Carpet Pads	Carpet and Rug Institute Green Label Plus Testing Program
	State of California Specification Section 01350, Section 9
Low-Emitting Materials, Flooring	FloorScore Program
Low-Emitting Materials, Furniture, IAQ	Environmental Technology Verification (ETV)
	ANSI/BIFMA X7.1-2007
	Greenguard™ Certification Program
Thermal Comfort	ASHRAE 55-2004—Thermal Comfort Conditions for Human Occupancy
	ASHRAE HVAC Applications Handbook, 2003, Chapter 4 (Places of Assembly)
Daylight and Views	ASTM D1003—07e1 Standard Test Method for Haze and Luminous Transmittance of Transparent Plastics
Mold Prevention	Building Air Quality: A Guide for Building Owners & FMs, EPA Reference 402-F-91-102
Green Cleaning	APPA Leadership in Educational Facilities: Custodial Staffing Guidelines
	California Code of Regulations Maximum Allowable VOC Levels
	Environmental Choice Certified Products
	Green Seal® Certified
	US EPA Comprehensive Procurement Guidelines
Green Cleaning, Equipment	California Air Resources Board

Appendix J

ABBREVIATIONS AND ACRONYMS

AE	Awareness & Education category (only for LEED for Homes)
AFV	alternative fuel vehicle
AIA	American Institute of Architects
ALP	ENERGY STAR Advanced Lighting Package
ANSI	American National Standards Institute
AP	LEED Accredited Professional
ASHRAE	American Society of Heating, Refrigerating, and Air-Conditioning Engineers
ASTM	American Society for Testing and Materials
BAS	building automation system
BD+C	Building Design + Construction (LEED AP credential and also a reference guide)
BEES	Building for Environmental and Economic Sustainability software by NIST
BIFMA	Business and Institutional Furniture Manufacturer's Association
BIPV	building integrated photovoltaics
BIM	building information modeling
BMP	best management practice
BOD	basis of design
BOMA	Building Owners and Managers Association
CAE	combined annual efficiency
CBECS	Commercial Building Energy Consumption Survey (by DOE)
CDL	construction, demolition, and land clearing
CFA	conditioned floor area
CFC	chlorofluorocarbon
CFL	compact fluorescent light
CFM	cubic feet per minute
CFR	U.S. Code of Federal Regulations
CI	Commercial Interiors (LEED CI rating system)
CIR	Credit Interpretation Request
CMP	Credentialing Maintenance Program
CO	carbon monoxide
CO_2	carbon dioxide
COC	chain of custody
COP	coefficient of performance
CRI	Carpet and Rug Institute
CS	Core & Shell (LEED CS rating system)
CSI	Construction Specifications Institute
CWMP	construction waste management plan
Cx	commissioning
CxA	commissioning agent or authority
DHW	domestic hot water
DOE	U.S. Department of Energy
EA	Energy & Atmosphere category
EBOM	Existing Buildings: Operations & Maintenance (LEED EBOM rating system)
ECB	energy cost budget

ECM	energy conservation measures
EER	energy efficiency rating
EERE	U.S. Office of Energy Efficiency and Renewable Energy
EF	energy factor
EPA	U.S. Environmental Protection Agency
EPAct	U.S. Energy Policy Act of 1992 or 2005
EPEAT	electronic product environmental assessment tools
EPP	environmentally preferable purchasing
ESA	environmental site assessment
ESC	erosion and sedimentation control
ET	evapotranspiration
ETS	environmental tobacco smoke
EQ	Indoor Environmental Quality category
FEMA	U.S. Federal Emergency Management Agency
FF&E	fixtures, furnishings, and equipment
FSC	Forest Stewardship Council
FTE	full-time equivalent
GBCI	Green Buildings Certification Institute
GBOM	Green Buildings Operations + Maintenance reference guide
GF	glazing factor
GHG	greenhouse gas
GPF	gallons per flush
GPM	gallons per minute
GWP	global warming potential
HCFC	hydrochlorofluorocarbon
HEPA	high-efficiency particle absorbing
HERS	Home Energy Rating Standards
HET	high-efficiency toilet
HFC	hydrofluorocarbon
HVAC	heating, ventilation, and air conditioning
HVAC&R	heating, ventilation, air conditioning, and refrigeration
IAP	ENERGY STAR with Indoor Air Package
IAQ	indoor air quality
ICF	insulated concrete form
ID	Innovation & Design category
ID+C	Interior Design + Construction (LEED AP credential and also a reference guide)
IDR	Innovative Design Request (only for LEED for Homes)
IEQ	Indoor Environmental Quality category
IESNA	Illuminating Engineering Society of North America
IPD	integrated project delivery
IPM	integrated pest management
IPMVP	International Performance Measurement and Verification Protocol
ISO	International Organization for Standardization
KW	kilowatt
KWH	kilowatt per hour
LCA	life-cycle assessment/analysis
LCC	life-cycle cost
LCGWP	life-cycle global warming potential
LCODP	life-cycle ozone depletion potential
LED	light-emitting diode

LEED	Leadership in Energy and Environmental Design
LL	Location & Linkages category (only for LEED for Homes)
LPD	lighting power density
MDF	medium-density fiberboard
MERV	minimum efficiency reporting value
MPR	Minimum Program Requirement
MR	Materials & Resources category
MSDS	material safety data sheet
M&V	measure and verification
NBI	New Building Institute
NC	New Construction (LEED NC rating system)
ND	Neighborhood Development (LEED ND rating system)
NIST	National Institute of Standards and Technology
ODP	ozone-depleting potential
O&M	operations and maintenance
O+M	Operations + Maintenance (LEED AP credential)
OPR	owner's project requirements
OSB	oriented strand board
PV	photovoltaic
PVC	polyvinyl chloride
REC	renewable energy certification
RESNET	Residential Energy Services Network
RFP	request for proposal
RP	Regional Priority category
SCAQMD	South Coast Air Quality Management District
SCS	Scientific Certification Systems
SEER	seasonal energy efficiency rating
SHGC	solar heat gain coefficient
SIP	structural insulated panels
SMACNA	Sheet Metal and Air-Conditioning Contractor's Association
SS	Sustainable Sites category
SRI	solar reflective index
TAG	Technical Advisory Group
TASC	Technical Advisory Subcommittee
TP	total phosphorus
TRACI	Tool for the Reduction and Assessment of Chemical and Other Environmental Impacts
TSS	total suspended solids
Tvis	visible transmittance
UL	Underwriter's Laboratory
USGBC	U.S. Green Building Council
VOC	volatile organic compound
WE	Water Efficiency category
WF	water factor
WFA	window-to-floor ratio
WWR	window-to-wall ratio
ZEV	zero emission vehicle

Appendix K

ANSWERS TO QUIZ QUESTIONS

CHAPTER 1: UNDERSTANDING THE CREDENTIALING PROCESS

Q1.1.   **A.** The new credentialing system is composed of five types of LEED APs at the second tier: BD+C, ID+C, Homes, ND, and OM.

Q1.2.   **A.** Yes, it is possible to sit for two exams in one day: the LEED Green Associate and any of the LEED AP + exams.

Q1.3.   **A.** Yes, LEED project experience is required, within three years of your application submittal date, in order to sit for any of the LEED AP exams, according to the LEED candidate handbooks.

Q1.4.   **C.** Be sure to remember USGBC is responsible for developing the rating systems, while GBCI is responsible for monitoring the certification process for projects and the credentialing process for professionals.

CHAPTER 2: INTRODUCTION TO THE CONCEPTS AND PROCESS OF SUSTAINABLE DESIGN

Q2.1.   **E.** All of the four options listed are environmental benefits of green building design, construction, and operational efforts.

Q2.2.   **B.** According to the EPA website, Americans typically spend about 90 percent of their time indoors.

Q2.3.   **A.** Thirty-eight percent of energy in the United States is used for space heating, followed by lighting with 20 percent of energy usage.

Q2.4.   **E.** All of the four options listed describe high-performance green building strategies.

Q2.5.   **B.** Risk is collectively managed in an IPD. The risks and rewards are both shared in an IPD project.

Q2.6.   **A.** Incorporating green building strategies and technologies is best started from the very beginning of the design process. Schematic Design is the earliest phase of the design process, and therefore the correct answer.

Q2.7.   **A.** It is important to remember LCAs not only look at the present impacts and benefits during each phase of the process, but future and potential impacts as well.

Q2.8.   **B and C.** LCAs include the purchase price, installation, operation, maintenance, and upgrade costs for each technology and strategy proposed.

CHAPTER 3: THIRD-PARTY VERIFICATION

Q3.1. **E.** It is not possible to register a project with a certification level indicated.

Q3.2. **D.** Refer to the USGBC website to download the Logo Guidelines at www.usgbc.org/ShowFile.aspx?DocumentID=3885.

Q3.3. **A.** GBCI is responsible for the appeals process as well as managing the certification bodies. It is best to remember USGBC as an education provider for the LEED rating systems they create, and GBCI as being responsible for the professional accreditation and project certification processes.

Q3.4. **A and C.** CIRs are submitted to the project's assigned GBCI certification body for review, electronically through LEED-Online. CIRs are limited to 600 words and should not be formatted as a letter. Since the CIR is submitted electronically through LEED-Online, the project and credit or prerequisite information is tracked; therefore, the CIR does not need to include this type of information. It is critical to remember CIRs are submitted specific to one credit or prerequisite.

Q3.5. **B and C.** Certification bodies are managed by GBCI and are assigned to a project team after registration, to assist with the process for a project seeking LEED certification, including the review of and response to CIRs. GBCI is responsible for the appeals process.

CHAPTER 4: UNDERSTANDING LEED

Q4.1. **A.** A project's LEED certification can expire, but only within one rating system: LEED for Existing Buildings: Operations & Maintenance. EBOM certification is valid for five years.

Q4.2. **C.** LEED for Commercial Interiors is best suited for tenant spaces within office, retail, and institutional project types, specifically tenant spaces that do not occupy an entire building. LEED CI goes hand-in-hand with the LEED CS rating system.

Q4.3. **D.** The LEED Core & Shell rating system is best suited for new construction projects where the developer/owner will occupy less than 50 percent of the leasable square footage.

Q4.4. **B and D.** LEED for Homes and LEED for Neighborhood Development both have different categories than the other rating systems. LEED ND has the following categories: Smart Location & Linkages, Neighborhood Pattern and Design, and Green Infrastructure and Buildings. LEED for Homes contains the unique categories of Location & Linkages and Awareness & Education.

Q4.5. **A.** LEED for Homes is the only rating system where a project can earn or lose points according to the number of bedrooms and the size of the house. Project teams use the Home Size Adjustment tool detailed in the LEED for Homes Reference Guide to determine if their project will have points credited or deducted based on the proposed size of the home.

Q4.6. **B.** Prerequisites are absolutely required just as minimum project requirements (MPRs) are for any project seeking LEED certification.

Q4.7. **B.** LEED for Existing Buildings: Operations & Maintenance is the best rating system for this project, as it involves only HVAC replacement and no other renovations. For the purposes of the exam, it is important to remember the project types applicable for each of the rating systems.

Q4.8. **A and C.** Although the credits within the LEED rating systems are now weighted differently in the new version, the rating systems were not reorganized. The five main categories still exist, but now the rating systems are based on a 100-point scale (except for the LEED for Homes, with 125 base points). Each credit is now weighted in correlation to their impact on energy efficiency and CO_2 reductions.

Q4.9. **C.** Ultimately, it is up to the project team to decide which rating system is best suited to their project. A LEED for Universities rating system does not exist.

Q4.10. **E.** The Reference Guide for Green Building Design and Construction (BD+C) is the resource for projects seeking LEED NC, LEED CS, LEED for Schools, LEED for Healthcare, or LEED for Retail certification.

Q4.11. **D.** USGBC consulted with NIST and the EPA's TRACI tool to determine the credit weightings by assessing carbon overlay.

Q4.12. **A and B.** Although the strategies listed will increase the first costs for a project, it is important to remember the life-cycle costs, including purchase price, installation, operation, maintenance, and upgrade costs.

Q4.13. **A.** Make sure to remember the point range scales of the LEED certification levels for the purposes of the exam.

CHAPTER 5: THE LEED® CERTIFICATION PROCESS SUMMARIZED

Q5.1. **C.** LEED NC, LEED CS, LEED for Schools, and LEED EBOM projects must include a minimum of 1,000 square feet of gross floor area, while LEED CI projects must include a minimum of 250 square feet of gross floor area.

Q5.2. **C.** LEED for Existing Buildings: Operations & Maintenance projects must serve one or more FTE occupant(s), just as with the other rating systems. LEED EBOM projects must also be occupied with all building systems in operations for the indicated performance period.

Q5.3. **B and E.** Be sure to remember each of the MPRs and how they pertain to each rating system, as posted on the GBCI website.

Q5.4. **A and E.** LEED NC, LEED CS, LEED for Schools, and LEED EBOM projects must include a minimum of 1,000 square feet of gross floor area, while LEED CI projects must include a minimum of 250 square feet of gross floor area.

Q5.5. **E.** All projects seeking LEED certification must commit to sharing five years' worth of actual whole-project energy and water usage data with USGBC and/or GBCI.

Q5.6. **B and E.** Appeals are electronically submitted to GBCI through LEED-Online for a fee, within 25 business days after the final results from a design or construction certification review are posted to LEED-Online.

Q5.7. **C.** It is also important to remember, although the Regional Priority category is a new addition to the rating systems, no new prerequisites or credits were created to include within the new category. The Regional Priority category offers bonus points for achieving existing LEED credits detailed in the other categories.

Q5.8. **B.** Although design reviews can be beneficial, points are not awarded until final review after construction.

Q5.9. **D and E.** Registering with GBCI indicates a project is seeking LEED certification. GBCI assigns a certification body to help a project team through the process and to answer any CIRs. Project registration can be completed at any time, although it is strongly encouraged to do so as early as possible. GBCI does not grant the award of any points regardless when registration occurs. Registration will, however, grant the project team access to a LEED-Online site specific for the project, but does not include any free submissions of CIRs.

Q5.10. **A and C.** Although registering a project requires some information, including contact information, project location, and indication of compliance with MPRs, a team must submit all credit submittal templates for all prerequisites and attempted credits during the certification application. Required supplemental documentation, such as plans and calculations, must be uploaded as well.

Q5.11. **C.** The earliest construction prerequisites and credits can be submitted, along with design prerequisites and credits, for certification review is after substantial completion.

Q5.12. **C.** It is important to remember that points are awarded only once the project team submits for construction review, not at the design phase certification review. Design-side review is optional and therefore not required.

Q5.13. **B.** Project teams have 25 business days to issue an appeal to GBCI after receiving the final review comments.

Q5.14. **B, C, and F.** CIRs can be submitted through LEED-Online, to the GBCI certification body assigned to the project, any time after registration. CIRs specifically address one MPR, prerequisite, or credit. Although the project administrator submits the CIR, the certification body response is viewable by all team members invited to the LEED-Online site for the project. CIRs are project specific, and therefore CIR responses will no longer be published to a database as they once were.

Q5.15. **A, D, and E.** Although it is strongly encouraged to begin the integrative design process and to incorporate green building technologies and strategies as early as possible in the design process, it is not intended to be an elaborate process. Value engineering should not be needed if the triple bottom line principles are applied.

Q5.16. **B and C.** Project teams working on LEED for Homes and LEED ND projects will work with USGBC for certification review.

CHAPTER 6: SUSTAINABLE SITES

Q6.1. **B.** Where a project is located and how it is developed can have multiple impacts on the ecosystem and water resources required during the life of a building.

Q6.2. **B.** In order to determine if a portion of land is a brownfield site, an examination is done via the ASTM E1903-97 Phase II Environmental Site Assessment.

Q6.3. **D and E.** Although sites near wetlands and bodies of water should be avoided, to comply with the Sustainable Sites credit, LEED projects should not be within 100 feet of wetlands or 50 feet of a body of water.

Q6.4. **A.** LEED for Neighborhood Development projects are encouraged to provide a higher street density with narrow streets interconnecting to prevent sprawl and to manage stormwater.

Q6.5. **A, B, and C.** According to the *Green Building and LEED Core Concepts Guide*, transportation is most impacted by location, vehicle technology, fuel, and human behavior.

Q6.6. **A, C, D, and E.** If a LEED project's site does not offer mass transit accessibility, and is therefore dependent on car commuting, it is best to encourage the occupants to carpool, offer alternative fuel-efficient vehicles, or incorporate conveniences within the building or on-site.

Q6.7. **A, B, and C.** Selecting a site near public transportation, limiting parking, and encouraging carpooling are all strategies to consider when working on a project seeking LEED certification. It is always best to redevelop a previously developed site, avoiding greenfield sites.

Q6.8. **C.** The key to reducing heat island effects is to avoid implementing materials that will absorb and retain heat. Deciduous trees lose their leaves and therefore are not the best decision. Xeriscaping to reduce evaporation, and increasing impervious surfaces to recharge groundwater, are great strategies for sustainable site design, but do not help to reduce heat island effects. They, in turn, reap the benefits of reduced heat island effects. Implementing paving and roofing products with a higher albedo, or SRI, is therefore the best answer to reduce heat island effects.

Q6.9. **F.** It is best to involve all the players related to designing and installing a green roof in a collaborative setting. Understanding the requirements of a green roof will indicate the team members required, especially what type of vegetation will be utilized. Remember, a green roof impacts the thermal elements of a building, structural integrity, stormwater management, and the coordination of construction trades.

Q6.10. **D.** Emissivity is the ability of a material surface to give up heat in the form of radiation. It may be helpful to remember emittance is the opposite of reflectivity. Infrared reflectivity applies to low-emissivity materials. Therefore, these materials reflect the majority of long-wave radiation and emit very little, such as metals or special metallic coatings. High-emissivity surfaces, such as painted building materials, absorb a majority of long-wave radiation as opposed to reflecting it, and emit infrared or long-wave radiation more willingly.

Q6.11. **A, B, and C.** The LEED rating systems recommend to combine the following three strategies to reduce heat island effects: provide shade (within five years of occupancy), install paving materials with an SRI of at least 29, and implement an open-grid pavement system (less than 50 percent impervious).

Q6.12. **A, C, and D.** Impervious asphalt does not allow rainwater to percolate through and therefore allows stormwater to leave the site, carrying pollutants and debris, heading to storm sewers and nearby bodies of water.

Q6.13. **B, C, and E.** Earning the Rapidly Renewable Material credit indicates the project was constructed with a percentage of building materials that can be grown or raised within ten years. For LEED compliance, credits are awarded for incorporating low-emitting materials used within the weatherproofing membrane.

Q6.14. **C and E.** Project teams can evaluate location and site-specific information prior to the beginning of designing a structure and the site, to determine the efficiencies of strategies and technologies for a green building project. These issues include the availability of mass transit and public transportation, and brownfield redevelopment. Strategies to reduce heat island effects, provisions for preferred parking, and technologies to reduce water use can all be addressed during the design process.

Q6.15. **D.** Access to ten basic services, such as banks, post offices, grocery stores, schools, restaurants, fire stations, hardware stores, pharmacies, libraries, theaters, museums, and fitness centers, is required to comply with LEED.

Q6.16. **B.** LEED requires a minimum score of 40 for low-emitting and fuel-efficient cars. Refer to www.aceee.org/ for more information.

Q6.17. **D and E.** Selecting products with the highest SRI values is best suited for compliance with LEED.

CHAPTER 7: WATER EFFICIENCY

Q7.1. **A and E.** Aerators and flush valves are the two most economically feasible options if fixtures cannot be replaced.

Q7.2.   **B and F.** Remember flow fixture and flush fixture types for the exam.

Q7.3.   **A, B, and E.** Turf grass poses a maintenance, economic, and environmental concern by the amount of watering it requires. Reducing pervious surfaces does not address saving water for landscaping, and from an environmental aspect, project teams are encouraged to *increase* pervious surfaces to recharge groundwater.

Q7.4.   **A, B, C, and D.** The site design strategies do not address increasing the density factor. Density can be increased by development design strategies, such as increasing floor-to-area ratio (FAR).

Q7.5.   **C, D, and E.** Installing open-grid pavers in lieu of asphalt minimizes the contributions to the urban heat island effect, as pavers do not absorb the heat from the sun as opposed to asphalt. By reducing heat gain, energy use is optimized, as the building has less of a demand for cooling loads. The pavers also allow stormwater to penetrate through to reduce runoff.

Q7.6.   **A, B, and C.** Process water is the water needed for building systems and business operations.

Q7.7.   **B, C, and E.** Blackwater is wastewater from a toilet. Remembering the different types of nonpotable water can help answer other questions about specific design strategies as related to water efficiency.

Q7.8.   **B and D.** Sometimes the process of elimination helps to determine the correct answers. Although captured rainwater is used for custodial uses, cleaning dishes and clothes is best with potable water sources.

CHAPTER 8: ENERGY AND ATMOSPHERE

Q8.1.   **A, B, and D.** Process energy is not included in minimum LEED requirements for the EA Minimum Energy Performance prerequisite. Process energy uses include computers, office equipment, kitchen refrigeration and cooking, washing and drying machines, and elevators and escalators. Miscellaneous items, such as waterfall pumps and lighting that is exempt from lighting power allowance calculations such as lighting integrated into equipment, are also categorized as process energy uses.

Q8.2.   **B, D, and E.** Refrigerants do not apply to boilers, fan motors, or variable-frequency drives, which eliminates answer options A and C.

Q8.3.   **C.** Remember each of the referenced standards and what each applies to. Remember to think "energy" every time you read "ASHRAE 90.1"!

Q8.4.   **B, D, and E.** Regulated energy uses include lighting, HVAC, and service water for domestic or space heating.

Q8.5.   **E.** It is critical to remember the details about refrigerants for the purposes of the exam.

Q8.6.   **B and D.** Remember, commissioning agents should be independent third parties to perform their responsibilities for the owner. A CxA is responsible for minimizing design flaws and assessing the installation, calibration, and performance for the main building systems.

Q8.7.   **A and C.** Using thermal storage and energy simulation helps to use energy more efficiently. Purchasing off-site renewable energy is a strategy to offset what cannot be produced on-site.

Q8.8.   **B, E, and F.** Passive solar design features and off-site strategies do not contribute to earning the On-Site Renewable Energy credit. Ground-source heat pumps do not qualify either, as they require power to function the pump.

Q8.9. **C.** Green power should be remembered with off-site renewable energy, as green power is purchased and not installed.

Q8.10. **B.** Think of when you go to purchase gas for your car, as you are charged by the gallon and not by the liter.

Q8.11. **C and E.** Although a commissioning agent will be responsible for verifying the installation, calibration, and performance of the cogen system, the strategy described in the question does not indicate any information involving a commissioning agent. The question does not indicate any renewable energy to be generated on-site, nor does it refer to any offsetting green power procurement.

Q8.12. **B.** Remember to make a flashcard to help remember this statistic.

Q8.13. **A.** Remember, it is advised to incorporate integrative design strategies as early as possible in the design process.

CHAPTER 9: MATERIALS AND RESOURCES

Q9.1. **C, D, and E.** Remember, preconsumer recycled content refers to scrap and trim material generated from the manufacturing process, but does not enter into the consumer cycle of goods. Preconsumer recycled materials are used to manufacture a different product than what it was originally intended for.

Q9.2. **A and D.** Regional materials, salvaged materials, and rapidly renewable materials are calculated as a percentage of the total material cost for a project for the purposes of LEED.

Q9.3. **B.** Rapidly renewable products can be grown or raised in ten years or less.

Q9.4. **B and D.** For the purposes of LEED, FSC wood products are calculated as a percentage of the total cost of wood products purchased for a specific project. Chain-of-custody documentation should be tracked and the certification number entered into the credit submittal templates for proof of compliance.

Q9.5. **A, C, and E.** The EPA's ENERGY STAR Portfolio Manager is used to compare energy use consumptions for similar-type buildings.

Q9.6. **B.** Landfills produce methane, a powerful greenhouse gas. Although methane can be captured and burned to generate energy, if it is emitted, it is harmful to the environment.

Q9.7. **B and C.** Cradle-to-cradle products can be recycled while cradle-to-grave materials are landfilled. Products with either or both preconsumer and postconsumer recycled content can contribute to earning the LEED credit.

Q9.8. **B and C.** Stormwater management plans are typically the responsibility of the civil engineer, while the energy modeling calculations are typically provided by the mechanical engineer.

Q9.9. **B, D, and E.** Although evaluating all of the vendor's procurement policies to ensure that sustainable purchasing procedures are in place could possibly contribute to earning an Innovation in Design credit, it is not required for compliance with any of the MR credits. The CEO's automobile choice is also not evaluated or assessed for LEED compliance.

Q9.10. **D.** FSC credit compliance requires the completion of a credit submittal template including invoice amounts and chain-of-custody certification numbers. Remember, all documentation is submitted for review via LEED-Online for all projects except LEED for Homes and LEED ND.

Q9.11. **C.** Furniture and electronics are not considered ongoing consumables.

Q9.12. **D.** Waste is calculated in tonnage for the purposes of LEED documentation.

CHAPTER 10: INDOOR ENVIRONMENTAL QUALITY

Q10.1. **D.** LEED requires a minimum of MERV 8 filters to be installed for compliance.

Q10.2. **B, E, and F.** Remember, the specifics of the referenced standards and what they apply to. Phenol-formaldehyde and urea-formaldehyde relate to resin-manufactured building materials. Knowing the requirements of each of the materials would have helped to eliminate answer option C. Option D is eliminated, as Green Spec is not currently included in the referenced standards addressed in the LEED rating systems.

Q10.3. **A, C, and D.** ASHRAE 90.1 = Energy! ENERGY STAR applies to energy-efficient appliances, products, and buildings.

Q10.4. **D.** Remember the specifics of the referenced standards and what they apply to.

Q10.5. **A.** Opening the windows is not sufficient means to eliminate contaminants, as the mechanical system (ductwork) and indoor environment needs to be flushed out with fresh air as well.

Q10.6. **B and D.** ASHRAE 55 defines the three environmental components that impact thermal comfort including humidity, air speed, and temperature.

Q10.7. **D.** Remember to read questions and answer options carefully to eliminate the incorrect answers and to depict the correct answer.

Q10.8. **A and F.** Remember the specifics of the referenced standards and what they apply to.

Q10.9. **C and D.** Remember to be cautious whenever you see "wood," as it might not always be applicable to FSC. Low-emitting materials typically apply to *new* building products and materials purchased and installed on a green building, not reused or salvaged products. Construction waste management would come into play only if the question addressed waste leaving the project site seeking certification, not recovering from another site, as that would be reuse.

Q10.10. **D.** 62 IAQ, IAQ 62!

Q10.11. **A and D.** Remember the BAIT tip to point out the trade-offs and synergies of increased ventilation strategies: better IAQ but reduced energy efficiency for mechanical systems to condition outside air.

Q10.12. **A and E.** Project specifications will give the contractor direction on how to comply with the IAQ credit requirements such as MERV filters, flush-out, and low-emitting materials.

Q10.13. **D.** Create a flashcard to remember this technical detail.

Q10.14. **A and C.** Remember ASHRAE 55 = thermal comfort and 62 = IAQ as both relate to ventilation system design.

Q10.15. **A and C.** Proximity to a shopping mall may increase satisfaction due to convenience, but not necessarily increase production as related to work. Carpooling and recycling are benefits to the environment and operations, not necessarily related to productivity or satisfaction.

Q10.16. **C, D, and F.** Remembering the strategies described in the EA and MR categories will help determine the correct answers. Review those flashcards!

CHAPTER 11: INNOVATION IN DESIGN AND REGIONAL PRIORITY

Q11.1. **C.** Earning exemplary performance is credit specific, so be aware of statements such as "regardless of which credit is being exceeded."

Q11.2. **C and D.** If unclear about ID credits, be sure to read through the Guidance on Innovation & Design (ID) credits on the GBCI website at www.gbci.org/ShowFile.aspx?DocumentID=3594.

Q11.3. **A.** A new green building project can earn the LEED NC certification and then earn the LEED EBOM certification during operations or a LEED Core & Shell building can be built and then earn multiple LEED CI certifications.

Q11.4. **A, C, and E.** Remember, the Regional Priority category is new but does not include any new credits. RPCs are earned by achieving existing LEED credits from other categories. Although earning a maximum of four RPCs is allowed, there are six opportunities available to choose from.

Q11.5. **D.** Although earning a maximum of four RPCs is allowed, there are six opportunities available to choose from for each zip code.

Q11.6. **A.** Regardless of how many LEED APs are on a project, only one point can be earned.

Credits

CHAPTER 1

1. GBCI. LEED Green Associate Candidate Handbook, June 2010 (2008), p. 7.

CHAPTER 2

1. Wikipedia website, http://en.wikipedia.org/wiki/Sustainability.
2. United Nations General Assembly, *Report of the World Commission on Environment and Development: Our Common Future* (1987). Transmitted to the General Assembly as an Annex to document A/42/427: Development and International Co-operation: Environment. Retrieved on 2009-02-1.
3. USGBC website, www.usgbc.org/DisplayPage.aspx?CMSPageID=1718.
4. GSA Public Buildings Service, "Assessing Green Building Performance: A Post Occupancy Evaluation of 12 GSA Buildings" (2008).
5. Environmental Protection Agency. *The Total Exposure Assessment Methodology (TEAM) Study* (1987).
6. GSA Public Buildings Service, "Assessing Green Building Performance: A Post Occupancy Evaluation of 12 GSA Buildings" (2008).
7. Heschong Mahone Group, "Daylighting in Schools: An Investigation into the Relationship Between Daylighting and Human Performance" (1999).
8. USGBC website, www.usgbc.org/DisplayPage.aspx?CMSPageID=1718.

CHAPTER 3

1. USGBC website, www.usgbc.org/DisplayPage.aspx?CMSPageID=124.
2. Ibid.
3. GBCI website, www.gbci.org/.
4. GBCI website. Disciplinary and Exam Appeals Policy, www.gbci.org/Files/Disc_ExamAppeals_Policy.pdf.
5. USGBC website, Logo Guidelines: LEED Logo, www.usgbc.org/DisplayPage.aspx?CMSPageID=1829.
6. USGBC, USGBC Logo Guidelines, 2008, p. 20.
7. Ibid.
8. USGBC website, Logo Guidelines: LEED in Text, www.usgbc.org/DisplayPage.aspx?CMSPageID=1828.
9. USGBC website, Logo Guidelines: USGBC in Text, www.usgbc.org/DisplayPage.aspx?CMSPageID=1831.

CHAPTER 5

1. USGBC website, www.usgbc.org/DisplayPage.aspx?CMSPageID=2102.

CHAPTER 6

1. USGBC, *Green Building and LEED Core Concepts Guide*, 1st ed. (2009), 30.
2. Ibid., p. 26.
3. EPA website, http://epa.gov/brownfields/about.htm.
4. USGBC, *Green Building and LEED Core Concepts Guide*, p. 31.
5. EPA website, http://epa.gov/brownfields/.
6. Ibid., p. 27.
7. Ibid.
8. Wikipedia website, http://en.wikipedia.org/wiki/Vehicle_Emissions.
9. USGBC, *Green Building and LEED Core Concepts Guide*, p. 28.
10. Ibid., p. 29.
11. Ibid., p. 30.
12. USGBC *LEED for Existing Buildings: Operations & Maintenance Reference Guide* (2008), Glossary, 494.
13. USGBC, *Green Building and LEED Core Concepts Guide*, p. 32.
14. Ibid., p. 33.

CHAPTER 7

1. USGBC, *Green Building and LEED Core Concepts Guide*, 1st ed. (2009), 39.
2. Ibid., p. 40.
3. USGBC *LEED for Existing Buildings: Operations & Maintenance Reference Guide* (2008), Glossary, 493.
4. USGBC, *Green Building and LEED Core Concepts Guide*, p. 41.

CHAPTER 8

1. USGBC website, www.usgbc.org/DisplayPage.aspx?CMSPageID=1718.
2. USGBC, *Green Building and LEED Core Concepts Guide*, 1st ed. (2009), 51.
3. Ibid.
4. USGBC, *LEED Reference Guide for Green Building Design and Construction* (2009), 146.
5. USGBC, *Green Building and LEED Core Concepts Guide*, p. 45.
6. Ibid., pp. 46–47.
7. Ibid., p. 49.
8. Ibid., p. 50.

CHAPTER 9

1. County of San Mateo, California, *San Mateo Countywide Guide: Sustainable Buildings* (2004), 3. www.recycleworks.org/pdf/GB-guide-2-23.pdf (accessed December 2009).
2. USGBC, *Green Building and LEED Core Concepts Guide*, 1st ed. (2009), 56.
3. USGBC, *LEED Reference Guide for Green Building Design and Construction*, (2009), Introduction, xi, 335.
4. USGBC, *Green Building and LEED Core Concepts Guide*, p. 55.
5. Ibid., pp. 54–55.

CHAPTER 10

1. Environmental Protection Agency, *The Total Exposure Assessment Methodology (TEAM) Study* (1987).
2. USGBC, *Green Building and LEED Core Concepts Guide*, 1st ed. (2009), 59.
3. USGBC, *LEED Reference Guide for Green Building Design and Construction* (2009), Glossary, 632.
4. Ibid., p. 495.
5. USGBC, *Green Building and LEED Core Concepts Guide*, p. 60.
6. Ibid., p. 61.
7. Ibid., p. 60.
8. Ibid., p. 62.
9. Ibid.
10. Ibid.
11. Ibid.

APPENDIX F

1. USGBC website, www.usgbc.org/DisplayPage.aspx?CMSPageID=220.

Index

Process (*continued*)
    certification, 41
    precertification, 44
  sustainable design, ix, 9, 171
  thermal, 85
  waste heat, 96
  water, 71, 80, 157, 176
Processed, 105, 108
Productivity, 11, 13, 122, 131, 132, 178
Professional exemption, 42
Programming, 14, 15, 163
Project
  Administrator, 35, 36, 41, 42, 174
  boundary, 37, 38, 39, 153, 154
  budget, 16, 17
  goals, 16, 103, 162
  registration, 41, 146, 155, 173
  schedule, 16
  site, 15, 31, 51, 52, 54, 58, 65, 71, 99,
      102, 105, 106, 107, 109, 119, 139,
      148, 162, 174, 178
  team members, 13, 16, 86, 106
Prometric, 6, 7, 145
Property boundary, 38, 39, 61
Protocol, Montreal, 88
Provider
  Green-e certified, 99
  Homes, 43
Public transportation, 9, 15, 51, 52, 55,
      63, 157, 159, 161, 175
Pump-and-treat methods, 54

R

Radiant heat flooring, 84, 93
Rain, 60, 67, 80
  acid, 55
  fall, 66
  garden, 66, 68
Rainwater, 60, 66, 67, 81, 175, 176
  harvesting, 68, 71, 72, 74, 76, 77, 78,
      81, 157, 159
Raised access floors, 129, 130, 133
Rapidly renewable
  materials, 106, 107, 108, 157, 161, 175,
      177
  products, 177
Rating system. *See also* LEED
  development, 20, 43, 58, 170
  selector, 41
  Ratio, 61
    building to site area, 38, 153, 154
    floor to area (FAR), 52, 176
REC. *See* Renewable energy credit

Recertification (EBOM), 44
Reclaimed water, 74, 77, 81
Recycled content, 105, 106, 107, 108,
      110, 136, 157, 166, 177
  assembly, 108
  postconsumer, 107, 119
  preconsumer, 107, 119, 135, 177
Recycling, 113, 114, 115, 135, 157, 165,
      178
Reference guides, 5, 27, 36, 106. *See also*
      LEED reference guides
References, primary and ancillary, 5, 17,
      145, 146
Reflectance. *See* Solar reflectance
Refrigerant, 88, 89, 90, 146, 165, 176
  enhanced, management, 104, 161
  management, 165
  fundamental, 29, 82, 88, 89, 161
Regional, 31
  Councils, 19, 139
  material, 106, 107, 108, 133, 135, 157,
      160, 161, 162, 177
  Priority, x, xi, 28, 29, 134, 137, 139, 140,
      144, 148, 161, 170, 173, 179
    category (LEED ND), 28, 172
    credit (RPC), 139
    variation, 31
Registration, 21
  project, 36, 41, 43, 44, 45, 146, 148,
      155, 172, 173
  fee, 36
  process, exam, 6
Regularly occupied areas, 131
Regulated energy, 87, 89, 90, 97, 176
Remediation, 52, 53, 54
  in situ, 54
  strategies, 54
Renewable
  energy, 31, 83, 86, 90, 96, 98, 99, 101,
      102, 103, 157, 169, 176, 177
  certificate, 170
  credits (RECs), 99
  eligible sources, 98
  off-site, 99, 102
  on-site, 99, 101, 104, 161, 165
    material, rapidly. *See* Rapidly
      renewable material
Request for information (RFI), 15, 20
*Residential Alternative Calculation
      Method Approval Manual*, 166
*Residential Manual for Compliance with
      California's 2001 Energy Efficiency
      Standards*, 166
Restore, 160, 161

Retail rating system. *See* LEED for Retail
Retaking LEED Green Associate exam, 149
Retro-commissioning, 84, 97, 102
Return air, 124
Reuse, 53, 75, 79, 89, 113, 115, 132, 157,
      159, 160, 161, 162, 178. *See also*
      Salvaged material and Material
      Reuse
*Review of ANSI/SHRAE Standard 62.1-
      2004: Ventilation for Acceptable
      Indoor Air Quality*, 146
Review
  permit, 15
  process, certification, 43
Risk, 16, 17, 36, 66, 163, 171
Roof, x, xi, 12, 13, 51, 60, 61, 62, 65, 66,
      68, 69, 70, 71, 85, 86, 92, 94, 101,
      159, 161, 175
  Green. *See* Green roof
  Material, 62, 64, 70, 175
  Vegetated. *See* Green roof
R-value, 17

S

Salvaged material, 108, 115, 177
SCAQMD. *See* South Coast Air Quality
      Management District
Schedule, study, xi, xii
Scheduling, LEED Green Associate
      exam, xii, 147
Schematic Design, 14, 37, 153, 163, 171
Schools rating system. *See* LEED for
      Schools
Scientific Certification Systems (SCS)
      Indoor Advantage, 123, 126, 170
Score, exam, 147
Scorecard, LEED, 41, 146, 155
SCS. *See* Scientific Certification Systems
Sealant, 123, 127, 135, 161, 167
Sedimentation
  and erosion control plan, 169
Sensor, 131
  faucet, 74
  fixture, 74
  light-level, 131
  moisture, 77
Setback, 52
Shade, 91
  Sun. *See* Sunshade
  vegetative, 65, 78, 175
Sheet Metal and Air Conditioning
      Contractors' National
      Association. *See* SMACNA

Trust, carbon, 166
Tuck-under parking, 62, 64
Turbine
  gas, 104
  wind, 87, 99
Turf grass, 176
Tvis, 170

U

Urban heat island effect, 61, 62, 176
Urea-formaldehyde, 123, 178
Urinal, 68, 71, 73, 74, 75, 76, 159
  Waterless, 73, 74, 75, 76
U.S.
  Code of Federal Regulations, 164, 168
  Department
    of Agriculture, 53
    of Energy, 168
  Environmental Protection Agency
      (EPA), 11, 31, 89, 146, 169, 181,
      183
  Fish & Wildlife Service, 164
  Geological Survey, 10, 71
  Green Building Council (USGBC), 3,
      10, 19, 21, 22, 25, 38, 83, 139, 170
    logos and trademarks, 20, 21, 22
    membership, 6
    regional councils, 19, 139
    website, 3, 5, 6, 8, 10, 11, 19, 20, 22,
      42, 83, 139, 146, 172
  USGBC. *See* U.S. Green Building
      Council

V

Value engineering, 16, 174
Variable Frequency drive, 89, 176
Vegetated
  cells, 80
  roof, xii, 13, 65, 66, 69, 159. *See also*
      Green roof
  swales, 78
Vegetation, 52, 66, 76, 160, 175
  native/adapted, 60, 62, 79
Vehicle

alternative fuel, 56, 168, 174
  fuel-efficient, 174
  high-occupancy. *See* high-occupancy
      vehicle
  hybrid. *See* Hybrid vehicle
  low-emitting, 56, 157, 161
  miles traveled (vmt), 57
  sharing program, 56
  zero emissions, 56, 164, 170
Vendor, 177
Ventilation, 9, 25, 83, 87, 89, 91, 122,
      124, 125, 126, 128, 130, 133, 134,
      135, 146, 158, 160, 161, 166, 169,
      178
  control, 129
  demand controlled, 126
  effectiveness, 89
  for Acceptable Indoor Air Quality,
      126, 166
  natural, 15, 85, 94, 160, 166
  trade-offs, 122
Verification, 19, 20, 22, 172
Views, 121, 131, 161, 167
Visible transmittance, 170
Vmt. *See* Vehicles miles traveled
VOC. *See* Volatile organic compound
Volatile organic compound (VOC), 110,
      111, 112, 122, 123, 124, 167, 170

W

Wall, 28, 86, 94, 161, 170
  Party, 37, 153
  Trombe, 73, 93
Waste
  disposal, 113
  diversion, 113
  diverted, 113
  management, 10, 106, 113, 115
  management, construction, 10, 106,
      113, 115, 117, 133, 157, 161, 178
  plan, 133, 168
  reduction, 11
    policy, 115
  solid, 11

Wastewater, 71, 74, 81, 161, 176
  treatment, 71
Water
  black, 74, 176
  body, 53, 55, 66, 71, 174
  efficiency category (WE), 28, 71, 84,
      148, 170
  efficiency, 13, 29, 31, 71, 72, 73, 74, 76,
      78, 80, 157, 160, 161, 175, 176
    indoor, 17, 71, 74, 75, 77, 157
    outdoor, 71, 76, 77, 79, 157
    process, 71, 80, 81, 157, 176
  gray, 74, 77, 81
  management, 148
  non-potable, 74, 81, 157, 159, 176
  potable, 60, 69, 71, 72, 75, 78
  process, 71, 80, 157, 176
  usage, baseline, 72, 73, 84
Waterless urinal, 73, 74
Watts, 97, 104
Weighting of LEED credits, 146
Wells, 60
Wetland, 53, 55, 66, 164, 174
Wheatboard, 107, 109, 123
Wind energy, 87, 98, 99, 101, 102
Window, 17, 86, 95, 106, 127, 128, 131,
      132, 160, 170, 178
  operable, 126, 129, 158, 160
  size and placement, 94
Wood, 78, 106, 108, 109, 112, 113, 116,
      119, 132, 135, 177, 178
  Certified. *See* Certified wood
  composite. *See* Composite wood
Workstation, 94, 133, 147, 148

X

Xeriscaping, 60, 77, 78, 157, 160, 175

Z

Zero emissions vehicle (ZEV), 56, 164,
      170
Zipcode, 139, 140, 179
Zoning, 39, 52